WHAT WILL I DO WITH THE REST OF MY

A Woman's Guide to Discovering Peace, Power and Purpose after 40

BRENDA POINSETT

DISCUSSION GUIDE INCLUDED

BRINGING TRUTH TO LIFE
P.O. Box 35001, Colorado Springs, Colorado 80935

OUR GUARANTEE TO YOU

The Navigators is an international Christian organization. Our mission is to reach, disciple, and equip people to know Christ and to make Him known through successive generations. We envision multitudes of diverse people in the United States and every other nation who have a passionate love for Christ, live a lifestyle of sharing Christ's love, and multiply spiritual laborers among those without Christ.

NavPress is the publishing ministry of The Navigators. NavPress publications help believers learn biblical truth and apply what they learn to their lives and ministries. Our mission is to stimulate spiritual formation among our readers.

www.navpress.com
ISBN 1-57683-151-5

Cover design and photo by Stephen Eames
Creative Team: Liz Heaney, Deena Davis, Lori Mitchell, Tim Howard, Angie Greenwalt

Some of the anecdotal illustrations in this book are true to life and are included with the permission of the persons involved. All other illustrations are composites of real situations, and any resemblance to people living or dead is coincidental.

Few of the names used in this book are the real names of the persons being described. Many names as well as details were changed to protect the identity of the person. New names were assigned to survey participants to distinguish them from other respondents who were quoted. Many Barbaras, Patricias, Nancys, Janes, Judys, and so on, participated. I'm sorry I couldn't connect the real name with every comment. It would simply have been too confusing.

Occasionally a composite of several stories is involved when that composite is based on survey responses and with what research shows to be true about midlife women.

When survey participants are quoted, I sometimes had to make some grammatical changes or add a word or two (as in transforming a phrase into a sentence) in order to add to the book's readability or to fit a format. I sincerely hope I didn't alter the intended message of the respondents. —Brenda Poinsett

Library of Congress Cataloging-in-Publication data number: 00-039437

Printed in the United States of America

1 2 3 4 5 6 7 8 9 10 / 05 04 03 02 01 00

To
Peggy Brooks
and
Pat McAlister,
two wise women
who helped me immensely.

CONTENTS

ACKNOWLEDGMENTS

I have never received as much help with writing a book as I have with this one, and I am deeply grateful. Many thanks to. . .

Gwen and Saundra. Your honest sharing prompted me to investigate the midlife growth of women.

Peggy Brooks and Pat McAlister. Bless you for reading and critiquing the entire manuscript. Knowing that you two were always there waiting for another chapter to read kept me writing. Your input was invaluable. I couldn't have written the book without you. That's why I've dedicated the book to you.

Selma Cobb, Jane Goodwin, Susan Miller, Sherry Deirth, Sandy Klaus, and Bob, my husband. You, too, read and evaluated portions of the book manuscript and proposal, and I appreciated your insights and comments.

Peggy Brooks, April Easter, Selma Cobb, Nancy Havill, Judy Pittman, Carol Cox, Jane Goodwin, and Jane Thompson, members of my discussion group. Your conversation and interaction were delightful and insightful. What fun it was to meet with you!

Patricia Avery, Susan Miller, Patricia Lorenz, Denise Mullis, Judy Lancaster, Judy Hickman, Barbara Wigger, Paula Maxheim, Nancy Jones, and Sandy Klaus. While you weren't members of the official discussion group, you provided me with lots of dialogue via phone, over tea, or through e-mail. It's always stimulating to talk with each one of you.

You who answered the survey—all 169 of you. I appreciate your willingness to take time to answer. Many of you who responded helped me further through phone calls, e-mails, and letters. Thanks for letting me share your stories.

Donna Williams, April Easter, Vicki Carol, Jeanna Bozell,

Susan Miller, Judy Mills, Pat Boyer, Vickie Wring, Eva Kirk, Mary Bess, Patricia Lorenz, Patricia Avery, Jackie Harmon, and Peggy Brooks. My survey list would not have been as broad or as large if you hadn't supplied me with lists of names of women to survey.

Carol Parkinson of Oakland City University—Bedford's library and the librarians at Bedford Public Library and Southwestern Baptist Theological Seminary's Roberts Library. How I depended on you for resources, and you were so good to find everything I needed.

Sandy Klaus, Peggy Brooks, Denise Mullis, Athalene McNay, Susan Miller, Mary Nell Boyer, Nanci McAlister, Liz Heaney, and Cathy Ingle, fellow members of Limestone Baptist Church and friends at Bedford's Free Methodist Church. Thank you for praying for me.

Cathy Ingle, Mary Maynard, and Jan Atkins. Thank you for your encouraging cards and notes. Each arrived at just the right time.

Sue Geiman, editorial director at NavPress. Thank you for your belief in the book and for your enthusiasm about this project.

Nanci McAlister, author relations at NavPress. Thank you for your encouragement and for being a person I could always turn to for answers to my questions. I work better knowing you are there.

Liz Heaney, my editor. Thank you for believing in the book from the time it was just an idea. Thank you for believing that I could write it. Thank you for pushing me to improve the manuscript. You bring out the best in me.

Bob Poinsett, my husband. Long ago, I nicknamed you Barnabas, which means "One Who Encourages." The name still fits. Thanks for encouraging me and for being patient through the writing process. And congratulations for being the only male on this list of acknowledgments!

When Liz first read the manuscript, she said, "I got the feeling I was listening in to a conversation of midlife women." From the list here you can see that the voices of many women were involved. I like to think of us as "the victory girls"—sharing our stories and pulling together to help middlescent women be all they can be. I thank God for each and every one of you, and the part you had in this book. May God bless you all!

CHAPTER ONE

AN INVITATION TO GROW

Why Do I Have So Many Questions?

I feel my life, like a river, moving steadily through the years and I am powerless to stop this process called aging. Questions plague me now in a way I have never experienced before and I feel restless, afraid.[1]

Paula Payne Hardin

Oh, no! Sandy told everyone I am fifty! I was dismayed as I looked at the promotional material she had created for my upcoming speaking engagement. *The women at her church will never want to listen to me—they'll think I'm too old.* Influential, quotable people are in their thirties and forties, not fifties.

In actuality I was a few months away from turning fifty. Sandy had looked at the birth year on my résumé without looking at the month. I was clinging to every day in my forties that I had left.

Turning thirty or forty bothers many people, but I breezed by those birthdays. I believed I still had time to dream, to be, and to do. But fifty said, "If you haven't done it by now, it's too late." All I could see before me was a settled life—even worse, a stagnant one.

My youngest child, Ben, would soon be leaving home. I was reluctant to let him go. Sometimes I would meet him at the door when he came in from school, throw my arms around him, and say, "I'm so glad to have a child coming home!" He must have thought I was crazy!

Sounds like a woman whose whole life was totally wrapped up in her children, doesn't it? Mine wasn't. I was a part-time college instructor, a writer, and a speaker; and I loved having children at home. I wanted my life to stay the way it was.

My days took on a wistful quality and my nights were filled with questions. *Is my life over? What am I going to do now? Will anyone value my opinion?* In the darkness I contemplated the future and didn't like any of the pictures I saw. But as I wrestled with my anxiety over aging, I felt something else. Something was pressing against my rib cage; it was as if something within me wanted to be released. I couldn't put a label on it—couldn't identify it. It was almost as if there were some force—dare I use the word *power?*—inside me wanting to be free.

I didn't mention my inner turmoil to anyone for fear I might have to tell my age! I probably would have gone on keeping it to myself—and missed out on some great discoveries—if I had not received two letters.

The Surprising Letters

The first letter was from a smart, talented professional colleague. She was so capable that I felt intimidated by her. Before mailing my letters to Gwen, I always checked and rechecked them for errors.

Somewhere along the line, our correspondence branched out beyond book ideas. We began mentioning personal details. She talked about problems with aging parents, and I talked about Ben leaving home. Then Gwen wrote that she had left her job as editor at a major publishing house. She didn't say why, only that she was going to school to pursue a graduate degree in theology. I assumed she may have been experiencing some burnout and needed some spiritual replenishment. Midway through the degree program, though, she switched to another course of study. She seemed at loose ends, as if she couldn't make up her mind what to do.

Her parents died, and she began experiencing physical problems. Menopause was proving to be difficult and she had developed arthritis in her knees. She wrote: "I think what's troubling me is an issue for many forty-five+ women. It's not the severity of the problems but the realization that my body is starting to break down and the future could hold a lot more of this. Also, with the death of my parents, the gut understanding that I am going to die and that few ways of dying are attractive bothers me."

I was surprised that a smart, savvy woman like Gwen would have such a hard time deciding what she wanted to do with her life and that she could feel so vulnerable about the future. I would have figured her to face the future with more confidence, but I could "hear" panic in her words.

The second letter was from Saundra, a longtime friend. Our friendship began when our children were preschoolers. Through the years I had admired Saundra's patience with her opinionated, quick-to-anger husband. Pleasant and compliant in personality, Saundra always tried to please Harry. I thought she epitomized the submissive wife the apostle Paul wrote about in Ephesians 5.

Harry adamantly insisted that "a woman's place" was in the home. Through the years, Saundra had stayed home except when she had to take temporary jobs during financially difficult times. Even then she thought of herself as a full-time homemaker, and so did Harry. Now in her letter, Saundra said, "I'm thinking of making some changes in my life. I have been married for twenty-eight years to a man who needs to control me. His methods of control have been verbal abuse and anger. Until recently, I was a willing enabler of this behavior. I thought I was being a good, submissive wife and that God would change Harry or somehow rescue me out of this life if I just kept on being a 'good wife.' Well, my husband hasn't changed, and I'm contemplating how I want to spend the rest of my life. My nest will soon be empty. I want to build a life that would give me satisfaction and meaning, like raising our children has given me. I want to stay in this marriage, but to do that I need to find work outside of my home to help bring perspective and meaning to my life. I'm thinking about going back to college and finishing my degree so I can embark on a new career. What do you think?"

What did I think? I was shocked. I had expected that Saundra would always be a full-time homemaker. She had always seemed so contented, at least from a distance. Perhaps if I had seen her on a day-by-day basis and corresponded more than once or twice a year, I wouldn't have been so surprised. It was such a change for her.

I couldn't help comparing my experience with Gwen's and Saundra's. All three of us were near fifty, and we were all wrestling with our futures. Who were we going to be? What were we going to do? What was the future going to be like?

I wondered, *Is what we are experiencing typical of women at midlife? Or could it be that our experiences were simply coincidental?* I headed for the library.

Middlescence

What I learned was that we were being invited to grow. Midlife, which the Bureau of Census labels the years 45 to 64,[2] is "a summons to grow and a challenge to change."[3] So that's what it was; we were experiencing growing pains!

C. G. Jung [founder of analytical psychology] recognized

> that what works for the adult person in the first half of life will not work for the second half. Each person's journey will unfold in a way that calls him or her to growth. Many books on midlife have been written since Jung first proposed that this period of adult growth is every bit as painful and unpredictable as the age of adolescence. This stage is variously referred to by authors as "midlife," "middle age," "middle years," or "the middle passage."[4]

Gail Sheehy popularized the idea of "passage" in her books *Passages* and *New Passages*. A passage or transition is "a period of change, growth, and disequilibrium that serves as a kind of bridge between one relatively stable point in life and another relatively stable but different point."[5] In the transition, we go from "one pattern of life that no longer 'fits' into a new pattern that is different."[6] This transition may involve so little emotional distress that it is barely noticed. On the other hand, it may be a time of wrestling and struggling, almost as if a birth is taking place. Indeed, one writer describes life transitions as "a time to give birth to our future and the quality of that future."[7]

Sheehy's label for the passage/transition between first adulthood and second adulthood is "middlescence."[8]

In adolescence, an earlier transition, we were separating from our parents, becoming autonomous, finding our own identity, and deciding what we were going to do with our lives. In middlescence, we leave young adulthood. For many of us, that involves redefining ourselves and deciding what we are going to do with the rest of our lives.

Ironic, isn't it? When we were in our late teens and early twenties, we asked ourselves, *What will I do with my life?* Assuming the answer covered a lifetime, we never thought we'd need to ask this question again. Now here we are at midlife, faced with the same question.

A Second Adult Life-Time

After turning forty-five, most of us will live for another thirty, forty, or even fifty years.

> A woman who reaches age fifty today—and remains free of cancer and heart disease—can expect to see her ninety-second birthday.[9]
>
> Even when all women, sickly or well, from every income group and every IQ level across the United States are averaged together, they can still expect at least thirty-two years and likely a span of forty or more years . . . after reaching their fiftieth birthdays.[10]

What do we want the quality of those years to be? A time of progressive decline, growing emptiness, and loss of vitality? Or a time of growth, fulfillment, and power? The difference depends on how we navigate the transition. Will we deal with its questions? Will we persist in looking for answers?

Now and Then

When I was an adolescent, I took my questions about my future to God; at fifty, I hesitated. When I was young I had a fresh, confident God-can-do-anything, all-will-turn-out-well kind of faith. At midlife, my faith was more realistic. It had been tempered by the stresses and disappointments of life. Experience had taught me that God's ways are not as understandable as I once thought. Following hard after God is no guarantee that our lives will turn out as we expect or hope.

Recently, I sat in a large audience where the speaker told us that if we just turn our lives over to Christ we would have happy homes. I found myself thinking, *I just don't believe that anymore.* I looked around at some women I knew in the audience—women of faith who did not have happy homes. Like Saundra, they had turned their lives over to Christ a long time ago and, from what I could tell, had served Him consistently. Like Saundra, who had waited for a happy marriage, they had waited for happy homes. And like Saundra, they were still waiting.

I also thought about Gwen. If she had told that speaker of her anxieties about her future, he likely would have responded by saying, "There's nothing to fear about the future; just have faith."

Cut and dried. Pure and simple. But experience had taught me things are rarely simple.

Was I wrong to be so realistic? Did my past experiences have something to do with my reluctance to embrace the future? God had disappointed me in the past. Could I trust Him with my future? I kept my questions to myself because I didn't want simplistic, adolescent answers for middlescent questions. I did, though, want to serve God and to please Him. I had learned from struggling with depression in my late thirties that I can't—nor do I even *want* to—live without God. Now I wanted to know: what does it mean to follow Christ as a woman of forty-seven, fifty-three, or fifty-eight? Does God have meaningful work for me to do? If He does, how can I discover it? How do I serve Him without youthful vigor and idealism? What kind of faith do I need for the second half of life?

Those Nagging Questions

Spiritual questions like these are characteristic of the middlescent transition, which takes place in the mind, the heart, and the spirit. It begins with:

- inner discontent
- hazy fears
- nagging questions
- impulses or pressure toward change
- seeing ourselves, our roles, or others differently
- disturbing dreams, or
- a sense that the old pattern no longer fits.

This is not to say that midlife growth cannot be precipitated by or exacerbated by concrete events in our lives: job loss, empty nest, death of friends and loved ones, menopause, the onset of a chronic illness, aches and pains, bifocals, even our birthday or someone's casual remark. (I was in a slump for three days after a twenty-year-old student said to me, "I hope I have your attitude when I'm your age.")

In our minds and our hearts we interpret these events and register their meaning, and the questions start coming. David J.

Maitland, a campus minister, chaplain, and teacher, writes, "For it is only as we are willing to live with the questions which our experience poses that it is possible for God gradually to make clear to us directions in which answers lie."[11]

Women live with the spiritual questions of middlescence in various ways. I began by articulating mine because I made no progress by keeping them to myself. They were filling my inner house. I needed to sweep it clean so I could give God space to direct me.

I started talking with other Christian women about my struggle—and yes, I started admitting how old I was! I brought up my questions in casual conversations with women I knew who would be candid. I organized discussion groups with other middlescent women. With the help of a friend, I developed a questionnaire and circulated it among Christian women ages forty-five to sixty-five.[12]

I sent the questionnaire to names gathered at a speaking engagement and to women in my address book. When these women responded, they sent me names and addresses of other women until I had 169 completed questionnaires from women ages forty-one to sixty-nine, who lived in twenty-four different states and in Germany.

I asked broad, open-ended questions because I wanted the women to express themselves; I wanted to "hear" what the respondents were thinking and feeling so I could connect with them. They must have wanted the same thing because many of them said, "Thanks for asking." Naturally, a survey of this nature wouldn't qualify as scientific, but that was not its purpose. It was an exploration process for me, a way to "live with" the questions I was asking.

I wanted to discover my own potential for growth, so I asked:

- What do you enjoy most about your present age?
- What kinds of power do you observe and admire in other women over forty-five?
- What kinds of positive changes have you made since turning forty-five?
- To what do you want to commit yourself over the next ten to fifteen years?

I wanted to know if their struggles were similar to mine, so I asked:

- What keeps you from making changes you would like to make?
- What spiritual challenges have you faced (or are you facing) since turning forty-five?

If they found solutions, I wanted to hear those too.

- What have you done (or, what are you doing) to meet your spiritual challenges?

While every woman's experience was unique, there were also similarities. The women's responses encouraged and challenged me. I began to see potential; I began to have hope that I could embrace the future.

There *Is* Life After Forty-Five!

When the tasks of questioning and exploring have lost their urgency and we are ready to commit ourselves to all that the next stage of life offers, a developmental transition ends.[13] As I gathered information and found answers, peace replaced my anxiety and I gained a vision of the kind of woman I could be in my fifties and sixties. There was a new woman inside me wanting to emerge, and I was ready to set her free.

The transition from young adulthood to middle adulthood may be relatively short or it may take several years (it did for me). We mull along, dimly aware that the route we have followed is no longer fulfilling. Yet we are reluctant to break the mold. We hold on to the familiar. The next stage, we tell ourselves, could never be as good as the one we are in. After all, it's familiar; the next is unknown.

Through exploring, I discovered I was wrong about my life being over. There *is* life after forty-five! Some of the best gifts of life come to us as we grow older (gifts that will make our lives enjoyable, productive, and meaningful). I would not have been able to discover those gifts—nor the woman I could be—without admitting what was bothering me and talking about my concerns with other women.

Wrinkles may come and gray hairs appear, but spiritual growth never has to end. As the apostle Paul said, "Even though our physical being is gradually decaying yet our spiritual being is renewed day after day" (2 Corinthians 4:16, TEV). When our spirits are healthy, everything is all lush and green on the inside. We thrive.

If your second adulthood is ahead of you, I invite you to come and grow with us. In this book, we'll tackle the spiritual questions common to many Christian women in their forties, fifties, and early sixties. I'll present the research I've gathered and the struggles and successes of the women I surveyed and talked with. In Part One we'll look at how we can let go of the things that may be holding us back from embracing all that the middle years offer; in Part Two we'll talk about partnering with God to build a vision of who we can be and what we can do; and in Part Three we'll find help for turning that vision into reality and becoming women of influence and power.

Will you join me? Together we'll make discoveries—about ourselves, about our future, and about the power and peace that is available to women over forty-five. I pray that you will discover, as I did, that God's best for you is yet to be.

PART ONE

LETTING GO OF WHAT HOLDS YOU BACK

CHAPTER TWO

BUT I'M NOT READY!

What If I Don't Want Another Life?

But I'm not ready! That is the protest I hear behind the refusal of so many of my interviewees in their forties to acknowledge they are not still twenty-eight. It's not me is the motto of a generation in collective denial of midlife.[1]

Gail Sheehy

A FRIEND GETS BIFOCALS.
Your mind seems fuzzy at times.
The couch looks awfully good at the end of the day.
You start buying slacks with elastic waists.

At first you ignore the signs. You don't want to admit you're getting older, that middle age is upon you. *The rain will fall somewhere else*, you think. *My friends are becoming middle-aged, but I'm not!*

One anonymous woman who answered my survey scrawled in large handwriting, "The changes I've made are not *age*-based!" (Her emphasis, not mine.) But she also added, "The changes I've made are based on professional and personal needs and the notion that *now* is the time. My children are grown and settled so I have more time for me!" Grown children? The sense that now is the time? Sounds like middle age to me!

When we know middle age is not going to miss us, our denial may change to out-and-out resistance. I call it the "oak tree" response.

HOLDING ON TO OUR LEAVES

I once lived in a house surrounded by trees, including seven oaks. Our first fall there I watched the leaves drop from the fruit trees, the maples, and the sycamores but not from the oak trees. This puzzled me. I wondered if something was wrong. At the time, I didn't know that oak trees hold on to their leaves longer than most trees.

Even in December, when fallen leaves from the other trees had been swept away by the wind, the oak trees were still holding on to their brittle brown leaves. Through rain and snow they clutched their leaves to their bosoms as if there could be no life for them once they gave up the leaves.

Like oak trees, many women hold on for dear life to what they have. We resist moving forward to the next stage of life. Certain that the way we live now is the *only* way to live, we hold on to our leaves—the facets of our lives as we now know them. We may resist for any of several reasons.

Security. We feel safe with what we know. Change is threatening and scary.

Unexplored territory. While others have navigated the middle years—and even say they enjoy them—those years represent unexplored terrain to us. We are uneasy and hesitant about the unknown.

Competence. We've managed to get a grip on being a young adult. We know how to do what we're supposed to be doing. We've got it down.

Loss of control. During middlescence, we begin to discover areas that we don't have as much control over as we once did. We gain weight more easily and have more difficulty taking it off; we have memory lapses and diminished energy; our hair begins to turn gray. No matter how well we have taken care of ourselves, physical and mental changes begin to occur.

Stereotypes. We feel the pressure of ageism—the belief that a person's worth and abilities are determined by chronological age. In our culture—and sometimes in our families and churches—certain things are assumed about us based solely on our age. Emerging from these assumptions are images of who a middle-aged woman is and what she should or should not do.

While many books are written on growing old gracefully and successfully, most people don't want to be perceived as "old." Because "middle age" is the last stop before "old," we try to hold on to the coveted label "young." We exercise religiously, we try not to look our age, and we resist telling how old we are. While some women will be in crisis situations when they enter midlife, most will be living full and productive lives or, at least, lives they are comfortable with.

Looking back, I can see that one of the reasons I held on to having a child at home was that it gave me a youthful connection. I felt good about having launched his older brothers; and yet, with Ben at home, I could cling to a younger image of myself. I didn't panic at the thought of his leaving. I had plenty to do. But I wanted to hit the pause button on the tape recorder of life and never let the tape move forward. I was happy with the way things were and I didn't want to wear the label "middle age."

Stuck in Resistance

A certain amount of resistance is normal, even healthy, as it can raise our awareness of the issues we need to face in order to successfully navigate middlescence. What we don't want to do is get stuck in resistance—like Margo, Sophie, and Grace.

Margo is depressed. She is still living in her bathrobe three years after her last child left home. She reads, watches television, and eats. That's it. She rarely leaves her house or interacts with others.

Sophie is a young-looking forty-eight-year-old who wouldn't be caught dead in her bathrobe, but she daydreams about moving to be near her only daughter, Carolyn, who lives in another state. Carolyn will soon be giving birth to Sophie's first grandchild, and Sophie spends hours fantasizing about getting an apartment near Carolyn and asking her husband to come visit her on the weekends.

Grace, who doesn't have children, is holding on to her way of doing things. Her early success in her company came because she was a stickler for details. Without Grace's realizing it, details became more important to her than the process and the personnel. Employees who have been there as long as Grace tolerate her preciseness because they appreciate her contribution to the company's success. Newer and younger employees, though, are impatient with Grace. They avoid working with her whenever possible. While Grace can't see her rigidity, she can see she is disliked. That hurts. When she was telling me how the younger employees treat her, she said, "It must be the difference in our ages."

Basically, these three women are refusing to admit that life continually changes and we need to adapt accordingly. When we find roles that we do well and feel competent in, or we find ways at being proficient, we feel comfortable and confident. When things change around us, calling for flexibility and growth on our part, we quietly fret. If only things would stay the same, then we would feel secure and sure of ourselves. We could tighten our grip on life and be successful and good at what we do. Change requires thinking, being alert, and stretching when we would rather coast.

While the responses of Margo, Sophie, and Grace may sound extreme, they represent what can happen if we get stuck. Without a doubt, middlescence has its challenges, but getting stuck means missing out on the possibilities offered by life's next stage. If we get stuck, we'll stop growing and maybe experience mental, emotional, and spiritual stagnation or decline.

How can we keep moving ahead? By opening our eyes to possibilities for the future. An attitude of expectancy doesn't solve all the perplexities of middlescence, but it can motivate and encourage us. We can cultivate an expectant attitude through prayer, conversations, and reading.

Opening Our Eyes Through Prayer

"Father, help me to be willing to look for possibilities for the middle years of my life." This prayer opens a woman to consider embracing the next stage of life and its potential.

Some women may not even realize they are free to make choices about their future—who they're going to be and what they're going to do. They've taken life as it comes, never questioning who they are or what is expected of them. As one of the women in my discussion group described it, "Instead of living, they are being lived." These women may need to pray, "Father, open my eyes to see glimpses of the woman I can be."

Why glimpses? Because middlescence is a process. It is more than likely that a complete picture of who we're going to be and what we're going to do will not come all at once. The picture will unfold as we explore and move through the middlescent passage. Praying indicates a willingness to allow God to form a vision in our minds.

Opening Our Eyes Through Conversations

While we resent the negative and limiting images that others have of middle-agers, we too may have some stereotypical views. Without our even realizing it, mental pictures—often unattractive—can contribute to our reluctance to move ahead. We may lump middle-agers and older people together instead of seeing them as individuals. I'm sometimes guilty of that.

A woman dressed in culottes, sturdy walking shoes, and thin

anklets initiated a conversation with me in the washroom at Burger King. As we dried our hands, she remarked about how uncomfortable the summer heat was, and then added, "But what can you expect at *our* age?"

I mumbled something in response and bolted for the door. *Our age? You've got to be kidding. Surely I'm not as old as you are. Don't pull that camaraderie bit with me just because you're assuming I'm postmenopausal.*

I didn't see us as having anything in common. Fact was, I tended to write off as boring most middle-aged women dressed the way she was. That's why I paid little attention to the woman under the hair dryer when I went to my hair stylist for a trim. In her white blouse, tan culottes, white socks, and black shoes, she faded into the background. I only noticed her because she was the one person there besides the hair stylist.

As she worked crossword puzzles while her hair dried, I automatically catalogued her as uninteresting. Then Corrinna, the hairdresser, introduced us and said, "You two have a lot in common."

"Oh?" I said. "How's that?"

"You are both Bible teachers."

To be polite, I asked the woman, who was out from under the hair dryer by now, "How long have you been teaching?"

"Just a couple of years. I've only been a Christian for five years."

My ears perked up! "Please tell me about your conversion," I said.

She told me she had become a believer at sixty years of age. When she told me that it was her eighty-year-old mother who led her to the altar, my eyes filled with tears and I sensed I was on holy ground.

She told me about what a hunger she had for God's Word after her conversion. She studied and pored over Scripture. "I just can't get enough," she said.

"How did you get started teaching the Bible?"

"After my conversion, I started attending a small church and became a part of the adult Sunday school class. By the questions I asked, my hunger for learning was soon evident to everyone. I also talked about how I studied and what kind of helps I used.

When the teacher moved away, they asked me to fill the vacancy."

She said all this with humility, as if she herself could not believe what God was doing in her life. As I listened to her, God's Spirit refreshed and renewed me—something I wouldn't have wanted to miss, but I came close because I stereotyped women who dressed in culottes. I judged them by what they wore rather than seeing them as individuals the way God would want me to see them and the way I wanted to be seen.

Many stereotypes about middle-aged women are prevalent in our culture—stereotypes that we may unconsciously buy into. But when we talk with women individually or in groups, we will be surprised, encouraged, and stimulated. As one discussion group participant said, "Being part of this group gets my 'juices' flowing." That's what we need. On our own, it may be difficult to catch positive glimpses of our future, but through conversations with other women we can begin to envision an exciting and meaningful future.

Opening Our Eyes Through Reading

While I initially went to the library to research why Saundra, Gwen, and I were experiencing unrest, what I read opened my eyes to possibilities for the future and helped break down my resistance to growth. I wanted to know more. I was particularly inspired by Gail Sheehy's *New Passages*, Letty Cottin Pogrebin's *Getting Over Getting Older,* and Frances Weaver's *The Girls with the Grandmother Faces.*

Naturally, I began noticing articles in magazines and newspapers about middle-agers. Perhaps the frequency of articles about women at midlife had always been there and I simply hadn't noticed until I was ready to see. I remember when friends of ours were expecting their first child. The husband said, "You know, I never paid any attention to parents and children before, but now I find myself always watching them." That's the way I felt about the coverage of midlife women, particularly those stories of women who defied cultural expectations.

Many of the articles I read claimed that today's middle-aged women are breaking the patterns; they are redefining middle age.

As the baby boomers continue to turn fifty, we're going to hear more stories of middle-aged comebacks, metamorphoses, late blooming, and spiritual transformations.

But baby boomers were not the first to challenge expectations. Midlife women were making changes, taking chances, and showing courage long before "baby boomer" was even a label, and their stories also helped me.

THE EXAMPLE OF STRONG, SPIRITUAL WOMEN

Mary Magdalene, Joanna, Susanna, and others who had been healed of evil spirits and diseases followed Jesus and supported Him out of their financial resources (see Luke 8:1-3). While the Bible doesn't mention the ages of Mary Magdalene, Joanna, Susanna, and the others, I am inclined to believe they were middle-aged. If they had young children, they wouldn't have been free to travel. If they were young women, it would have been scandalous for them to travel with Jesus and twelve male disciples. Scandal isn't even hinted at in the biblical account. They had to have been tough, flexible, and courageous to travel with Jesus; those words are not typical of the way we usually describe middle-aged women.

Years later, in the early twentieth century, Mildred Cable and Francesca and Evangeline French displayed similar traits.[2] After twenty-one years of routine missionary work in China, they believed God was calling them to China's great Northwest. There were cities there where the name of Jesus was unknown.

When others learned of the determination of these three single women to go, some said, "There are no fools like old fools." Some of their coworkers were convinced that these women had misinterpreted the call of God in their lives: why leave important, successful school work to go off on some harebrained scheme of roaming vast deserts to look for tent dwellers? They went anyway.

Their journey was difficult. They traveled for months by cart, which rumbled and jolted over uneven, muddy mountain roads. On one occasion they were stuck in three feet of mud. They settled in a town nicknamed "the city of prodigals" because it attracted a large criminal element and many transients. This city became the center of their ministry, and they branched out from there. Through their pioneer work, China's great Northwest was opened to the gospel.

Corrie ten Boom's life was routine, too, until she was past fifty. In her book *The Hiding Place,* Elizabeth Sherrill described Corrie as "broad of frame and sensible of shoe." If I had known her, I would probably have written her off as a "culottes woman."

Corrie's life was suddenly transformed when she became a daring secret warrior against the Nazis during World War II. She hid Jews in her home, was caught, and experienced the horrors of concentration camps. She learned many spiritual lessons during this time that she later used in a worldwide ministry of comfort and counsel.

When we read stories about biblical, historical, and contemporary middle-aged women, we nurture our belief that God calls and uses us. We may not do the same kinds of things as the Galilean women, or as Mildred Cable, Francesca and Evangeline French, and Corrie ten Boom, but that's not the point. We can take heart from their adventurous spirits, the growth they experienced, the courage they showed, and the purpose their lives exemplified. They followed God's call despite odds, risks, and hardships.

Contrast their lives with the anonymous woman mentioned at the beginning of this chapter who insisted the changes in her life were not age-related. To the question, "Have you made a positive change in your life since turning forty-five?" she checked "no." To the question, "Would you like to make a major change?" she checked "no." To "What spiritual challenges have you faced since turning forty-five?" she answered, "None. I remain steadfast in my faith and spirituality."

I'm sure that if Corrie ten Boom, Mildred Cable, Francesca and Evangeline French, and the Galilean women were here, they would be the first to tell us their lives were difficult and even frightening at times, but they knew their lives counted. Let's not be afraid to grow. Let's look to the future with expectancy and hopefulness. Let's be open to God's call.

Letting Go of the Leaves of Young Adulthood

Sometime in early spring, when my family and I were still living in the house with the oak trees, I looked out my living room windows and noticed that the oak leaves were gone. Where did they go? When did it happen? When I walked to the mailbox, I stopped and looked closely at one of the trees. I could see new growth. Buds were forming. The oak trees had let go of their leaves and were ready for new life.

One day I realized I was no longer resisting middle age. Through reading, interacting with other women, and praying, I had let go of the leaves of my young adult life. I heard God's call to growth and I discovered that I could be a happy middle-aged woman.

CHAPTER THREE

UNFULFILLED EXPECTATIONS

If My Earlier Dreams Weren't Achieved, Why Bother with New Ones?

Too many people approach the second half of their lives with regrets over the first half. ("I should have spent more time with my family." "I should have developed better relationships." "I should have . . .") Regret is a tough emotion to live down: it haunts you in ways that will sap your strength and inspiration to go on to better things. So, one of the first things you need to do in halftime is make peace with your first-half set of issues.[1]

Bob Buford

WHAT DREAMS DID YOU HAVE WHEN YOU WERE IN YOUR TWENTIES?

Did you assume that you would know the love and companionship of a good man?

Did you expect to have an enduring and happy marriage?

Did you dream about having children, about the kind of mother you would be and how your children would turn out?

Did you fantasize about the kind of house you were going to live in or the kind of lifestyle you were going to have?

Did you expect to be able to always count on fellow believers for comfort, support, and guidance?

And, in all of your visions of the future, did you see yourself as competent and successful; happy and secure?

Many of the women I surveyed spoke of unfulfilled expectations, shattered dreams, hurts, and disappointments:

- "I struggle with why I've never really been loved by a man."
- "My husband's request for a divorce was the last thing in the world I was expecting."
- "For years I longed to pray with my husband and discuss spiritual matters with him, but I've given up that idea."
- "The spiritual challenge I've faced since turning forty-five is seeing the ways I failed my children spiritually during their growing-up years."
- "Ever since childhood I've dreamed of living in a grand old house. My husband and I have bought several antiques through the years, but living in an old house continues to elude me. Sometimes I feel ashamed for having such a materialistic goal, but on occasion I find myself moved to the point of tears when I realize this goal is likely to remain unattainable."

- "I was very disappointed to find a lack of support for single women in the church or from Christian friends. I had to realize that my spiritual needs were not necessarily of concern to anyone else."
- "I've gone through a period of depression because of being hurt by Christians in different areas of my life—things I would have expected from the world, but not from brothers and sisters in Christ."

Many spoke of deep disappointment in themselves:

- "I have always been dissatisfied with myself and therefore have always identified myself way too much with my teaching job. When it went well, I was okay. Now my career is on hiatus and I've found that not only am I still dissatisfied, I'm a total stranger to myself. I've never felt that I was very interesting or clever, and now I'm without any identity at all! I feel like 'No Face' from Dick Tracy!"
- "I have had several physical problems since turning forty-five, which certainly make me dissatisfied with myself and I think have kept me from being the wife, mother, and Christian that I would like to be."
- "I have always battled 'being' and 'doing.' I continue to try to redo the tapes of my childhood, which gifted me with the double-edged sword of perfectionism that helps me excel and yet demands more than is humanly possible at times. I need to recognize and celebrate all that is—to continue to look at the glass half-filled and rejoice rather than beating myself up for not doing 'it' better, faster, more perfectly."
- "In my desire to be all things to all people, at times I fail everyone. I'm disappointed that at my age the library books are overdue, I lose things regularly, I'm not organized, and I'm always late. Sometimes I think, 'You're almost fifty years old and haven't grown up yet.'"
- "My lack of faith, my feelings of sadness, and wanting to cry all the time are the spiritual challenges that bother

me the most. Sometimes I've felt that my life has no purpose, and I don't like myself very much."

- "I have low self-esteem, which gives me more of a negative attitude than I want to have. I'm never satisfied with myself."

We have hurts and disappointments at any age; but when we were younger, we also had the hope that things could still change. Around the bend . . . on another day . . . past the current hurdle, all the pieces of life were going to fall in place and we would live happily ever after.

When we enter middlescence and those things haven't happened, we may find ourselves frequently sighing over yesterday's hurts and disappointments. We catch ourselves saying, "If only . . ." or "If I had it to do over again . . ." We dwell on what might have been or what will never be.

If we don't make peace with our past and ourselves, we won't be able to dream new dreams because we are filled with doubt and pessimism. We think, *If earlier dreams weren't fulfilled, why bother with dreams for the future? Why make choices and take the chance of being disappointed again?*

The Importance of Dreams

The dreams and expectations we had as we left home and made our way in the world gave us a sense of how we wanted our lives to turn out. They fed our hope and propelled us forward to new and unfamiliar territory. Our dreams and expectations fueled our energy and gave us goals to work toward.

For the same reasons, we need dreams and expectations for the second half of life. The Bible says, "Where there is no vision, the people perish" (Proverbs 29:18, KJV). Without a dream, hope dies. Without a mental picture of who we can be or what we can do, effort diminishes. The quality of the remainder of life is related to our dreams. "It is vision that creates and sustains our hopes, and it is vision that won't allow us to settle for less than we can attain."[2]

How can we make peace with our past and with ourselves in order to dream again?

Accept What We Can't Change

Acceptance sounds passive, like resignation. But it is an active process. Acceptance means to receive willingly and favorably. It is an affirmative response—saying yes to *reality* with the mind and the heart.

This is not to say that some of our dreams still can't come true or that we shouldn't try to pursue dreams we had in our twenties. Neither is it too late for us to change in some areas—it's not too late to learn to get those books to the library on time! Self-dissatisfaction can be healthy when it motivates us to change what we can. I love the wisdom found in the serenity prayer:

> God, grant me the serenity
> To accept the things I cannot change;
> Courage to change the things I can;
> And the wisdom to know the difference.[3]

Once we recognize and accept what we can't change, our vision clears. We can see the things we can change. We can see possibilities we didn't know existed. Our energy rises. We make peace with ourselves and with life. We gain inner harmony and strength to meet the challenges and demands of life.

I like the way Sarah Ban Breathnach puts it in her book *Simple Abundance.* She writes, "When I surrender to the reality of a particular situation—when I don't continue to resist, but accept—a softening in my soul occurs. Suddenly I am able to open up to receive all the goodness and abundance available to me."[4]

For some people, acceptance may come quickly. They see what needs to be done and quickly arrive at an affirmative response. For most people, though, acceptance will be a process of surrender and affirmation.

Sweeping Our Inner House Clean

Surrender means sweeping our inner house clean. That means getting into the nooks and crannies and sweeping away the dirt or swiping at the cobwebs thickened with accumulated dust.

The Bible tells us to cast all our cares upon God for He cares for us (see 1 Peter 5:7). "All our cares" includes our concerns over the past and our dissatisfaction with ourselves. To break the past's magnetic power over us, we need to surrender it to God. That means we give Him all our hurts, disappointments, broken dreams, and unfulfilled expectations. At the same time, we release all the accompanying emotions that weigh us down.

Here are some ways you can sweep your inner house clean:

Articulate your hurts, disappointments, and self-dissatisfaction. God already knows these things, but when you verbalize them, you help release them.

Pray specifically rather than in generalities such as, "Dear God, help me to trust You," or "I just wish You would take all of this away," or "Help me to accept myself as I am." Tell God what your hopes and expectations were and how you have been disappointed. Tell Him about your struggle and how it has affected your life. Then say something like this: "I have carried this disappointment far too long. It is weighing me down and is coloring my perspective of the future. I don't want to carry this weight any longer. I give it to You."

If you have been hurt by fellow Christians, members of the clergy, or others, describe to God what a weight this hurt has been and your weariness in carrying it. Then say something like: "This hurt is very hard for me to release. Rather than asking You to forgive them, I really want to ask You to punish them. But I want to do what is right, and so I give You my anger and resentment over what happened. I give You my ill feelings. I forgive the people who hurt me. I give You the past. I release it to You."

If you are holding yourself accountable because of past failures or shortcomings, these may be keeping you from seeing a bright future. This, too, must be surrendered. Jesus already died on the cross for whatever sins we've committed. To continue to be bogged down by past indiscretions and errors is to say that His death was not enough. It's time to let the past go. To do so, you can pray something like this: "As much as it pains me, I have to admit that I'm not the woman I thought I would be by now. I've made mistakes. I've done things I wouldn't want my friends or family members to know about—things I can't even believe I am guilty of. These indiscretions are never far from my mind, yet I'm so tired of the mental wrestling. Father, I want to be free. I release my past to You, and I accept the forgiveness You provided through Your Son Jesus."

Adopt a prayer. If you find yourself unable to articulate your disappointments, you might want to borrow the words from someone else's prayers. Jesus' last prayer gives us a picture of trust. "Father, into your hands I commend my spirit" (Luke 23:46, KJV). *Commend* means "to entrust, to deliver with confidence, to give as a deposit for trust or safekeeping." We can deposit into God's hands our self-dissatisfaction, our frustrations over the past, and our broken dreams by praying Jesus' way.

"Father, into Your hands I commend my view of myself. I relinquish my view, and I want You to reveal to me how You see me."

"Father, into Your hands I place my frustrations with the changing nature of life. I look for the opportunities You are going to give me to grow with each change."

"Father, into Your hands I deposit the past. Sometimes I was keenly disappointed and even disillusioned at times, but the past is the past. I give it to You, and I am going to leave it with you. I am trusting You to help me live the rest of my life with hope and expectancy."

As long as we hold on to the past or to our dissatisfactions, peace will elude us. When we surrender the past and all that we find wrong with it, God will renew our energy and increase our hope.

Add a ritual. My friend Peggy, a counselor who helped me with this book, says that some women may need a ritual to help them surrender their hurts to God. Here's what she suggests.

- Write your prayer of surrender, express your feelings, and then lock the prayer up or throw it away.
- Visualize your burden in a basket and put it in a closet you seldom open. Close the door firmly as you leave.
- Scribble your hurts on scraps of paper and burn them one by one.

At times I've been surprised by how fast prayerful surrender works. I experience almost immediate relief. But most times, it takes days of soul work to sweep my inner house clean. Like any housework, I think the degree of difficulty depends on how long I've put off tackling the job!

FILLING THE VACUUM THROUGH AFFIRMATION

There is a comforting exhortation found in the book of Isaiah: "The LORD says, 'Forget what happened before, and do not think about the past. Look at the new thing I am going to do.'" (Isaiah 43:18-19, NCV). Once we've released the past (once we've swept our inner house clean) the relief we feel is so great that we may be tempted to stop there. The relief and immediate peace we experience makes us feel as if our problem of perspective is solved, but it isn't.

Our surrender creates an inner void. The surrender has cleared up the inner space for dreaming, but if we don't fill it, the old haunts—the ones we released—may come back and bring more with them!

Jesus warned us about this kind of thing in a strange parable He told (see Matthew 12:43-45; Luke 11:24-26). He told about an evil spirit leaving a person and traveling over dry country, looking for a place to rest. If the evil spirit can't find a resting place, it says to itself, "I will go back to my house." The evil spirit goes back and finds the house he left clean and all fixed up. Then he goes out and brings home seven other spirits to live with him. As a result, the person who swept his house clean is in worse shape.

To avoid this, we need to ask God to fill the vacuum. We can pray something like this: "Today, Lord, I see myself as being free of hurt and disappointment. I see myself as being optimistic about life again because You will help me. I see You smiling in approval of me as I make this effort to see what You have for me to do and to be in the next stage of life. I believe You have a purpose for me, and I am going to trust You to reveal it to me. In Your way and in Your time, You are going to speak to me. You are going to give me a vision of the woman I can be because I have cleared my channel of receptivity. I anticipate hearing from You, and I look forward to what You have to say."

Or you might want to affirm yourself or your future through giving thanks repeatedly. Gratitude is an avenue to acceptance. We can give thanks for the changing nature of life. "Thank You, Father, that life changes. Thank You for the opportunity to grow with these changes. Thank You for the mental and spiritual stimulation that comes with change."

We can thank God for who we are: "Father, I thank You that I am who I am. I thank You that You have given me everything it takes to serve You. I thank You for the knowledge that I do not have to be perfect or competent in all areas in order to have a meaningful life. I want to always please You."

We can fill the vacuum with the truth by memorizing, studying, or meditating on God's Word. Even the hunt to find those passages related to self-acceptance, life, forgiveness, and release can be helpful because our search implies a willingness to surrender. Here are some passages to start with. From these, you can find others.

- But by the grace of God I am what I am. (1 Corinthians 15:10, KJV)
- For to me to live is Christ, and to die is gain. (Philippians 1:21, KJV)
- I have learned, in whatsoever state I am, therewith to be content. (Philippians 4:11, KJV)
- And we all, with unveiled face, beholding the glory of the Lord, are being changed into his likeness from one degree of glory to another. (2 Corinthians 3:18, RSV)
- And the world passes away, and the lust of it; but he who does the will of God abides for ever. (1 John 2:17, RSV)
- But there is one thing I always do. Forgetting the past and straining toward what is ahead, I keep trying to reach the goal and get the prize for which God called me through Christ to the life above. (Philippians 3:13-14, NCV)

These prayer exercises are not simple or easy, but if we earnestly use them, over time we will be able to make peace with ourselves and with our past. As writer Barbara Bartocci acknowledges, "Letting go is something all of us have to go through. We leave neighborhoods we know and love. We marry and have children. We win promotions. We lose jobs. Our parents die. Our children leave the nest. In every experience, happy or sad, there's a need to let go of what *was*. Until we do, we can't appreciate what *is*."[5]

Neither will we dream about what *will be*. When we accept what we can't change, our wistful "If *only* . . ." will be replaced with a hopeful "What *is* . . ." or an even better "What *if*. . . ." Now we're talking possibility, otherwise known as dream language.

CHAPTER FOUR

TRAPPED!

How Can I Think About What I Want When Others Need Me?

At forty-eight years old, I'm straining at the bit to go on to new endeavors in my life and can't because I still have my precious fifteen-year-old to finish raising. I have to remind myself that God makes all things complete in His time.

Athalene, a survey respondent

JOANNE, WHOSE E-MAIL ADDRESS IS "MAMA BLACK," WOULD be the first to say she's a people-pleaser. At forty-five, she is the mother of four children, ranging in ages from nine to nineteen. She not only wants to take good care of her children, she wants them to be happy. She works hard at running the household and keeping everyone on schedule. Even though her employment takes her away from home three days a week, she earnestly tries to "be there" for her kids, so much so that when she takes a day off and visits her sister she feels guilty. Even when she and her sister are garage-sale shopping, something Joanne loves to do, inside there's a persistent, nagging thought: *I ought to be home; my kids need me.*

"Women value relationships,"[1] and we have many relationships at midlife. Like Joanne, some of us still have children living at home. Some of us have grown children living on their own, with whom we relish having contact. Many of us have sons- and daughters-in-law and grandchildren. We have spouses, friends, parents, sisters, brothers, coworkers, and fellow church members. At midlife, our circle of relationships is quite large and, consequently, so is our circle of concern. Caring and relationships go together.

CIRCLE OF CONCERN

One woman wrote, "My greatest challenge has been maintaining my faith and spiritual focus while parenting teenagers and young adults." The problems of older children are often more heartrending than the problems of children in younger years. These problems may have serious consequences, and they come at a time when we must change our parenting styles if we want to influence our children.

Many middle-aged women become parents to their parents or other elderly relatives who need assistance. The average American woman will spend more years caring for parents than for children.[2] This requires time and energy and can take an emotional toll, as the following words reflect.

- "My late mother and mother-in-law, and now my aunt, had deteriorating brain functions, which necessitated someone else taking over their care. Besides caring for their needs and affairs, I have had to painfully watch them lose their independence."
- "This year has been very stressful for me. The doctor told our family that my mother has Alzheimer's disease, and I knew that I was unable to care for her. I felt very guilty for putting her in a nursing home."

Some women are sandwiched in the middle, caring for both their children and older relatives, or they have hurts at both ends of the spectrum. Meeting these responsibilities becomes even more difficult if complicated by personal needs.

- "In 1991, at age fifty-four, I was diagnosed with breast cancer and had a mastectomy. In the same year my mother moved into our home. In December 1996, she had a stroke, which affected her thinking. We had no choice but to put her in a nursing home. In March 1997 our twenty-year-old granddaughter moved into our house. My husband and I have had to adjust to all of these circumstances."
- "My husband and son do not relate to each other. My father died after several years of senile dementia. Eleven days before that, my father-in-law died. Two months later my only sister died suddenly at age forty-nine. My son (only child) developed several major illnesses and hasn't been able to work. He's twenty-six and still home with us. I'm going through menopause."

One woman wrote: "My middle son, a pastor, developed MS. He was forced to retire on disability after only five years of being a pastor. My mother had to enter a nursing home." This woman wanted to quit her job so she could help both her son and her mother, but she couldn't do that because she was divorced and had to work in order to support herself.

In addition to caring for those we love, many women have

employers to please, deadlines to meet, and bills to pay. Midlife bulges with the weight of relationships and responsibilities.

WHAT FREEDOM?

Some women enter middlescence feeling like their lives are inflated like a tire to the maximum pressure. As Ann wrote, "Where's that free time that empty-nesters are supposed to have? I gave up my free time to baby-sit my grandchildren so my daughter could pursue her dreams." Ann doesn't begrudge this; she adores her grandchildren. What she would like to do is give up the part-time job that she no longer enjoys. Her husband, though, doesn't want her to because her income adds extras to their life. Ann feels trapped and tired.

A woman may feel that she's unable to hear enough, be enough, and do enough for the people she cares about, so she bristles when anyone—including this author—starts talking about potential, purpose, and dreams. She wonders, *How can I think about what I want—or what God wants—when my time and energy have to be devoted to others?*

Caring for others can be physically and emotionally stressful, no matter how much we love the people involved. Jan told me that for her the stress is almost intolerable. She wants to simplify her life and eliminate many of the less important details, but she finds it hard to say no to the demands others make. She says, "Their requests are not unreasonable, but they are about what *they* want." She wrote, "My husband and married children have busy, complex lives, and their needs must be coordinated with mine. God has given me the gifts of teaching and administration, so I want to teach Sunday school and to lead Bible studies, and so on. I feel called to work in God's kingdom in these areas but setting reasonable priorities is difficult for me. Meeting the needs of others keeps me in distress."

If you feel the needs of others pulling at you, you may feel annoyed, frustrated, fatigued, angry, and guilty or resentful. One woman expressed it this way: "For the past few years, I've felt that my life serves no purpose except as a slave to others. I feel very used up by my family, especially my husband, and now it's like, well, your job is done, we don't have time for you anymore."

In addition, you may wonder where God is, or if what you're going through makes any sense. You may feel hopeless because you can't see an end to your circumstances. You may compare yourself to others who have a much easier situation.

When it seems like everyone is wanting a piece of you, it's understandable that you might feel used up and worn out. But if left unchecked, these feelings can swell and fill up your dream space and distract you from listening for God's voice.

Breaking Through

If you want to break the stronghold that the needs of others have on your dream space, you might have to ask yourself some tough questions.

Are there changes I can make or initiate that will give me more time? For example, are there any tasks and responsibilities you can delegate? Athalene's family consumed much of her time and energy until she learned to set some boundaries about what she was willing to do and what she expected others to do. She wrote,

> I felt it was God's best for me to be a stay-home mom while the children were in the nest. I devoted myself to the care and advancement of the kids and my husband. I now feel it is time to devote myself more fully to work I truly enjoy. That means I am no longer a service object around the house. I began by telling my husband and children (two young adults and a fifteen-year-old) that I would be doing more of what I desire to do and less for them. However, that did not mean I would be living in an unorganized, untidy house. They were expected to pitch in with housework (without verbal prompts) and to be responsible for their own calendars. I even made certain we have a master calendar, so we can all know what's going on for each of us.
>
> When I limit how much I will do for my family, I have more freedom to develop into the individual God created me to be.

A family conference, or several conferences, may be necessary when you are caring for an older or ailing family member. With a "this is *our* problem" and "what can *we* do about it" approach, you can ensure that caring for Dad or an invalid sister is a group effort. Cooperation is easier to gain when you are *specific* about what needs to be done. Carol Sue made this deal with her brother: "If you will take care of paying all the medical bills, I will take our parents to all their doctor's appointments."

Your own standards may get in the way of soliciting help. Some of us have a "perfectionist gene" that resides right beside our "people-pleaser" gene. Whether it's the care of our aging mother or the laundry, you want the job done right. You may be reluctant to ask your husband or brothers or children to help, because they would not do it in the same caring, efficient way you would—obviously, the way it ought to be done!

It wasn't perfectionism that kept Thelma from asking for help, it was a promise. When she got married, she promised Ed she would always help him care for his widowed mother. By the time she was forty-seven, Thelma was being a supportive wife to Ed, helping him manage their rental property. She was also the mother to her two sons, ages ten and seventeen. And, as she had promised, she was caring for her husband's mother who lived next door, plus caring for his aunt who lived across the street. When her mother-in-law had a stroke that brought on mild paralysis and major pain because of complications with medicine, Thelma ended up in the hospital with caregiver's burnout. During her hospital stay, Thelma had time to think. She wrote:

> I came to realize that I could not take care of my mother-in-law anymore, but I was afraid to tell Ed. I had promised him before we got married that I would always help him care for his widowed mother. I was afraid our marriage would be over if I admitted I could not keep my promise. When I finally got the courage to tell Ed, he almost flipped. He reassured me that his mother's situation would never have that effect on our marriage. Immediately Ed became involved, and we set about finding outside help for his mother's care.[3]

"Caregiving has traditionally been a woman's role. . . . Societal pressures and expectations have trained generation after generation of women to put others' needs before their own."[4] That doesn't mean that we should never question the role or question aspects of the role. Help may be available; but to get it we may have to challenge the situation and ask ourselves if there are any changes we can initiate.

Am I willing to seek the insight of others? You may think, *There's nothing I can do*, but others may be aware of resources or alternatives hidden from our view. If you feel overwhelmed, with no end in sight, you might find insight and encouragement from one of the following groups:

- Support groups for caregivers
- Support groups for hurting parents
- Support groups for grandparents as parents
- Sunday school classes
- Bible study and/or prayer groups
- Counselors

Carileen wrote, "I attend a weekly couples' Sunday school class with other parents with children in their twenties. Many of us struggle with the same questions. The fellowship has kept me going through these times."

With the help of a counselor, Joni learned that she could care about others *and* have a life of her own. "I went through counseling because of worry and distress over my son's behavior, which made me take a look at my life. To achieve fulfillment I resumed activities that I enjoy, like gardening. I learned that I can even enjoy going to the movies or out to eat by myself!"

Am I hiding behind the "have-tos" in my life? David Maitland, the campus minister, chaplain, teacher, and author whom we met in chapter 1, says that those who have the most trouble with midlife growth are those whose focus has largely been on others' well-being. After responding to the needs of others for so long, they often have difficulty taking their own needs seriously.[5] Perhaps you have been in a "pleasing mode" for so long that you don't know what you want. It may seem unnatural (even selfish) to think in terms of what you want to be and do.

It's not selfish to know who you are and what you want; it is being self-aware. Being aware of who we are—our strengths *and* our weaknesses—is an important part of spiritual growth (see Psalm 119:59; 139:23; Lamentations 3:40; Haggai 1:7; 2 Corinthians 13:5). We are not to think more highly of ourselves than we ought, but we are to think of ourselves with "sober judgment" so that we can see how we may contribute to the body of Christ (see Romans 12:3-8). Self-awareness enables us to recognize our particular gifts. In the same paragraph in which Paul reminds us to bear one another's burdens, he also says that each one should test his own actions and carry his own load (see Galatians 6:1-5). We need balance.

Nancy reminded me of this when I asked her how she could care for her mother who was dying, her much older husband who was daily growing more dependent, and handle her job as vice president of a credit union. She told me, "If I don't take care of my health, I don't have energy to help my mother or my husband. If I don't think about what I want, I don't have anything to give them. My dreams stimulate me. They keep me from being swallowed up by the responsibilities of care-giving."

Some of us may already know who we want to be or what we want to do, but we're afraid to venture into new territory. We tell ourselves, *As long as others need me, I can't pursue my dreams.* This way we don't have to take risks or be adventurous.

Do I think of my situation as temporary or permanent? When we're heavily involved in caring for others or dealing with challenging teens, it's easy to generalize. We think life will always be like this; we will never have any time to be and to do. But children won't always be dependent; young adult children will eventually mature; our parents won't always be with us.

Look for ways you might grow or benefit from your circumstances by asking, *What is God wanting to do with me in this situation? What is He wanting me to learn now that will benefit me in the future?* As she cared for her mother and husband, Nancy said that God told her, "You're not being asked to give; you are the receiver."

She said, "My mother's long illness and death brought me

to a childlike trust in God; I totally depended on Him and I experienced the most profound peace I have ever known. I received just what I needed as I needed it. This is a gift that will continue to serve me well as I love my husband while his needs change dramatically and as I guide him through the end of his life."

What God teaches us when we are caring for others will serve us well for the days ahead when we pursue our dreams. When we're ready to redefine our lives, the world doesn't step back and say, "Go for it." There are always hurdles (things to do and conditions to respond to). Life is about compromises. There are times when we are the ones who are cared for, and times when we do the caring.

What's Important

Our lives are intertwined with people we love—people who enrich our lives. Sometimes their needs are greater than at other times, but we wouldn't want to be without those relationships. When I bluntly asked Nancy if caring for her husband held her back from pursuing her dreams, she said, "What is more valuable than being with someone?"

Catherine Marshall said that after her marriage to Leonard LeSourd, she had to start all over with motherhood. She had raised a son, and now she undertook the rearing of a second family—Leonard's children by his first wife. Catherine pointed out that this slowed her writing a great deal. A novel she was working on took nine years instead of three or four. She wrote, "The new responsibilities in addition to my writing have taken all my resources of physical and spiritual strength and have given back a full life. . . . The bumps and bruises and turbulence are part of the price you pay for life's richness."[6]

Life for women is not either/or (either we have relationships *or* we follow our dreams). It's about intertwining the two. We can think about what we want and what God wants even when others need us. We can grow and gain from the experience. So give yourself permission to dream about who you can become and what you can do. Don't put any pressure on yourself; don't compare yourself with others; and don't set any limits. Just dream and see what kind of woman God calls you to be.

CHAPTER FIVE

OH, MY ACHING BACK!

Will I Ever Feel Good Again?

Being healthy contributes immensely to my sense of enjoyment of my age. My state of health seems to affect my entire outlook overall and how I approach/receive each day. I know this is true for any age, but I rarely thought about good health until middlescence.

April, a survey respondent

"AT AGE FORTY-FIVE, I WAS A MESS: ANXIOUS, NERVOUS, AND depressed. Much of this was due to poor health," wrote a forty-nine-year-old woman. Who would argue that our health affects our sense of well-being? The women I surveyed connected good health—and a positive future—with traveling, learning, enjoying friendships, helping other people, working, self-confidence, and spiritual growth. As they looked ahead to retirement and hoped for longevity, some were making physical fitness a goal for the next ten to fifteen years.

OUR CHANGING BODIES

We should all practice good health habits, but even with the best of efforts we may encounter physical problems. "The midlife woman is part of a group that begins to have health problems, something which increases with age."[1] Physical changes make us more vulnerable to some diseases; the consequences of past lifestyles or health habits may catch up with us; unrecognized stress or environmental factors, as well as other variables—many still to be determined—take their toll.

According to the research, 10 to 25 percent of midlife women will experience a difficult menopause.[2] This was true for Ruth. At first, her hot flashes were mild, but within a year they became so intense she couldn't sleep through the night. "I'd wake up, and the sheets would be damp. I'd throw the covers off, and then I'd freeze. After four weeks of this, I just sat in bed sobbing hysterically."

Of course, her lack of sleep affected her ability to concentrate. She could no longer comprehend the long, technical reports she had to read at work. This worried her: "I've always been on top of things at work. What if I lose my job? What will I do?"

Research also indicates that chronic illness arises with age.[3] Peggy, the counselor mentioned in chapter 3, was diagnosed with a chronic illness when she was forty-one. She had gone to the doctor to find out why her fingers were often infected. After a series of medical tests, she was told she has scleroderma. Her doctor told her, "Scleroderma is not a fatal disease. You will be able to handle all the symptoms as they come up. What you will mostly be aware of is not getting any wrinkles as you age."

Peggy thought, *Gee, I can handle this!*

The doctor suggested that she write the Scleroderma Foundation for more information. She did and discovered she was facing an ugly, disabling, and eventually fatal disease.[4] There was no known cure.

Health problems have a way of spilling over into other areas of life, affecting us not only physically but mentally, emotionally, and spiritually as well.

The Fall-Out

When our health is failing or we are experiencing pain and discomfort, our well-being can become our primary focus. Both the physical condition itself and our attention to it require energy that we could use to pursue our dreams.

- "I would like to be more active at church and in the community, but chronic fatigue syndrome is keeping me from it."
- "My energy level is low because of lupus. The last couple of years it has gotten really hard to keep everything going. I have to be in bed about ten hours out of twenty-four, so the rest of the time is hectic. I wish I had more time for myself, my grandchildren, and for ministry to others. I also love to paint, read, do stained glass, and write poetry, but I've had to lay these hobbies aside."
- "Since health problems occurred, I have been dissatisfied with my life's accomplishments, but I lack the energy to make any changes."

Many of us breeze through our young adult years, but then we hit midlife and the illusion of control is ripped away. One forty-six-year-old woman I know recently had a mammogram. She's always had a clean bill of health, so she was unprepared when the radiologist informed her that he was recommending a biopsy in her left breast because of calcification in the cells. Even though the biopsy report was that the cells were benign, she told me, "I've never worried about my health, but this was a wake-up call."

If we have never encountered this kind of impasse before, we may feel a sense of panic. We wonder, *Will the future mean more of the same?* We may become pessimistic. If we have a chronic illness, we may wonder, *Why plan for a future when I have so little control over the present?* We may become anxious, fearful, hesitant.

- "I fear the future. I worry over my health and my husband's health."
- "Spiritually I struggle with the fears that come with growing older and having health problems. I do not want to be defined by my physical status."
- "I would like to get back into a career that I feel could be helping others and contributing more to society. I have a health problem that prevents me from being able to get medical insurance, so I feel like I'm stuck."

Some of the women I surveyed noted that since turning forty-five, physical concerns were affecting them spiritually. Here's what some of them said.

- "I was diagnosed with lupus. I lost a much-loved sister to cancer . . . I've had major surgery twice. My mother went to a nursing home this year. All of this sounds physical, but it's also spiritual. Why me, Lord? Why now? When will it stop?"
- "Since turning forty-five, I have had several physical problems that certainly make me dissatisfied with myself and keep me from being the wife, mother, and Christian I would like to be."
- "My chronic fatigue syndrome has caused me to feel a lack of purpose."
- "God has put me through some very serious health problems that only He can cure. If He chooses not to, I am faced with the challenge of accepting that also."

- "Maybe due to the stresses of a new career or middle-age crisis or lack of trust—I have developed irritable bowel syndrome, which I find both physically and spiritually embarrassing."

Health problems may cause us to question things we've never doubted before. We may wonder, *What is God doing? I thought He loved me—if He does, why is this happening to me?* Or we may think, *If I really had strong faith, this wouldn't be happening to me.*

As one respondent wrote, "Physical problems affect everything you do, from relationships to serving the Lord to doing your daily tasks at home and at work." Poor or deteriorating health may narrow our focus, reduce our energy, and dampen our outlook about the future. But it doesn't have to be this way. We have options. There are things we can do. We can challenge our thinking, take action, seek healing, use what we have, and watch our focus.

Challenge Our Thinking

One woman wrote, "The constant hormone fluctuations of this age can cause diminished faith, floundering, dissatisfaction with self, and a lack of inner peace in the course of a day, let alone a year or five years."

That's a lot to attribute to hormones. If a woman dismisses all these problems as hormonal, she might miss out on some valuable insight she could gain from exploring these issues.

Another woman in her forties wrote, "I'm moodier, so I know I'm pre-menopausal." Age-wise, she's right, but that may or may not be the reason for her moodiness. Many things may be going on in the life of a woman in her forties and early fifties—the empty nest, concern over adolescent or young adult children, aging parents, changes in the workplace—all of which can affect a woman's emotions. Before attributing our emotional state to declining hormones, it's wise to look at what else is happening in our lives.

One woman I surveyed said she admired women who "recovered from menopause," as if it were a disease. It isn't. Menopause is a God-designed (natural) life event that is problematic for a small percentage of women. And menopause doesn't last forever; our bodies adjust to the changing hormone levels. It may mean the end of reproduction, but it does not mean the end of living.

"Cross-cultural studies also tell us that menopause is not experienced the same by all women. Expectations play a major role in symptom reporting, and those who perceive menopause to be an adverse event report more symptoms. . . . It is also clear that in societies where women acquire social, religious, or political power in the postmenopausal years, symptoms are minimal."[5]

Aging, too, has taken on disease proportions. While it is true that our susceptibility to certain diseases increases with age, aging itself is not a disease. It, too, is a part of God's gift of life. Surely, God must have meaning for us to discover as our bodies age. Part of my quest in researching and writing about midlife is to discover what God might have in mind for an aging, postmenopausal woman. If we blame our lack of purpose or vision on our physical problems, isn't it possible that we are limiting God and His ability to help us grow?

Take Action

Many of the women I surveyed reported they were taking steps to understand their bodies and make positive changes that would result in increased well-being.

- "I am going to classes so I can understand Crohn's Disease and its effects."
- "I have taken charge of my compulsive overeating by attending Overeaters Anonymous. It has changed my life on every level—physical, emotional, psychological, and spiritual."
- "I'm learning about and getting involved with 'wellness' and 'prevention.'"
- "At age forty, I lost over one hundred pounds and made a commitment to God—with His help, I would never put it back on. Now, twenty-six years later—at age sixty-six—I have kept it off! It has given me much more self-confidence in many areas of my life."

- "I came to realize at about forty-five that the Lord was trying to bring me to a more disciplined life through illness. I have changed the way I eat and exercise."
- "I changed from a tight schedule and being tired most of the time to a pace I felt I had more control over."

Even menopause can be affected by what we do. Various studies show that symptoms of menopause can be affected by diet, exercise, and attitude.[6,7] Hot flashes, for example, were half as common in physically active women as in those who were sedentary.[8]

Seek Healing

When we associate pain with aging, we may not seek God's healing because we assume this is the way it has to be. But until we've asked God to heal us, we shouldn't assume He won't. Praying invites God to work in our lives and makes us receptive to His power.

A friend of mine with a chronic condition stopped by to tell me of her impending operation. Although this operation had been in consideration for some time, the doctor's final word had left Vivian visibly shaken. As if she were trying to summon all her courage, she heaved a big sigh and said, "I just have to accept this as God's will for me. I guess He intended a life of suffering for me."

Anyone is bound to say something like that under stress, so I was careful to be gentle with my inquiry. "Have you asked God to heal you? Maybe this is a time for God to receive glory, not a time for you to suffer. Asking will let you know."

When Jesus heard that Lazarus was sick, He said, "The final result of this sickness will not be the death of Lazarus; this has happened to bring glory to God, and will be the means by which the Son of God will receive glory" (John 11:4, TEV).

Neglecting to ask is to do God a disservice, for it might be the very opportunity He wants to reveal His power and His glory.

But what happens if we ask for healing and God says no? If this is your situation, acceptance may be the key to your willingness to embrace the future. Acceptance, as you recall from chapter 3, involves surrender and leaning on God for help.

Guidance for accepting our pain or physical limitations can be found in E. Stanley Jones' signature prayer. Jones believed in the power of acceptance; he called it victory through surrender.

I am Yours, and this thing concerns me,
so this is Yours, too.
I surrender it.
Tell me what to do about it.[9]

As you say the prayer, you will want to name "this thing" that concerns you. In fact, you may want Jones' prayer to serve as an outline for your own prayer.

I am Yours, Lord.
A long time ago, when I was a child,
I gave my life to You.
I am a Christian;
I bear the name of Your Son, Jesus.
Our relationship has been long and strong
And now I find myself in distress.
I am constantly in pain
and experience debilitating fatigue.
I asked You to heal me
many times, and You did not.
I know, though, because I'm yours,
my fibromyalgia concerns You.
I give it to You.
I surrender it to You.
As Jesus deposited His life into Your hands,
I surrender my health to You.
And as I do,
I ask You to show me how to live
with what I can't change.

Don't be surprised as you articulate this prayer (it will be much more effective if it is said out loud) to find yourself becoming emotional. Your health, or the loss of it, is an emotional issue as well as a spiritual and physical one. Terry discovered this when she surrendered her rheumatoid arthritis to God. "I was filled with sadness," she said, "and it all surfaced as I prayed. I had lost my career, my control over my life, my future as I had envisioned it, and my sense of wellness. I had to let that go or I don't think full surrender could ever have been possible. This was a terribly difficult step for me; but as I reached out, God responded with the gifts of comfort and peace. Eventually, with God's help, I learned to live with what I couldn't change."

In 2 Corinthians 12:7-9, Paul talks about his thorn in the flesh, his messenger from Satan. Paul didn't say what the thorn was. Some scholars say the thorn was malaria, because the Greek word for *thorn* could be interpreted as "stake." The malaria fever in that region of the world was like a stake pounded into the forehead when it occurred. Other explanations are epilepsy, severe headaches, poor eyesight, carnal temptations, or the continual persecution Paul had to endure in preaching the gospel. Paul asked God to heal him. He prayed for the thorn to be removed. Instead of removing it, the Lord said, "My grace is sufficient for you, for my power is made perfect in weakness" (2 Corinthians 12:9). In the peace that follows surrender, we can count on God's grace to help us.

Use What We Have

When I showed Pat, a retired school administrator, this book's list of questions, she looked up when she got to, Will I ever feel good again? Emphatically, she said, "I can tell you the answer to this question. It's NO!"

She was admitting to something many of us have to adjust to: our physical well-being at fifty-five and sixty-five is not what it was at twenty-five or thirty-five. Loss, though, doesn't have to be our primary focus. To prevent this, we need to think about what we have to give, what we can do with the time, energy, and strength we do have. Some will have more strength than others, but we will each have *some* strength. What will we do with it?

Even with the thorn in his side, Paul continued to serve God.

His letter to the Corinthians when he described his prayers for the thorn to be removed was written on his third missionary journey, near the beginning. Paul finished that journey, went to Jerusalem, spent time in a jail in Caesarea, finally headed toward Rome, was shipwrecked on Malta, ministered during his time in prison in Rome, and then had more years of ministry before his final imprisonment in Rome. Paul had that amazing ability to be content in all situations (see Philippians 4:11). I might add, he also had the ability to minister in all situations.

After the Mayo Clinic diagnosed Peggy's scleroderma, she asked God to heal her. God did not heal her, but He gave her grace to bear it. She prayed for guidance on what to do with the years she had left. She said, "I told God that my desire was to be used up by Him. I wanted meaningful work to do."[10] God's answer led her to work with people; that's when she began her training to become a counselor.

WATCH OUR FOCUS

Pain has a way of grabbing and keeping our attention. Consequently, we may be tempted to become self-absorbed and avoid all other concerns. We may cease thinking in terms of possibilities—what we can be and what we can do. Instead we figure it's futile to dream.

One thing about being over fifty that I still haven't adjusted to—and don't know if I want to—is being in conversations where the talk centers around aches, pains, doctors, and medicine. It's almost as if the rest of the world or God's purposes cease to exist. When our health becomes the object of our worship and devotion, personal and spiritual growth ceases, yet growth is still possible.

Peggy told me, "Without goals, I believe I would either be living in fear of what the future might hold for me or I would be so busy fighting fear that I would have little energy left for anything else. I would probably be depressed and have a negative, even bitter, attitude toward life. I would also be fearfully waiting for the next symptom to appear.

"When I asked God for direction, set some goals, and began working toward them, I was choosing to walk away from a life of fear and bitterness. I was totally aware that I was at a crossroads with this disease. I would either choose to live a full, interesting life for as long as I was physically able, or I would simply surrender to scleroderma and use it as an excuse for a miserable, fearful existence. Eventually I will probably have to surrender to this disease; in the meantime, I am so thankful God has directed me to exciting, energizing work that I find meaningful. There is no doubt in my mind that I will live a longer, more meaningful life because of the road I have chosen."

Peggy claims 2 Corinthians 4:16 as her "scleroderma verse": "Even though our physical being is gradually decaying yet our spiritual being is renewed day after day" (TEV). I find it interesting that Paul wrote this verse in the same letter that he prayed for his thorn in the flesh to be removed. No matter what physical infirmities we experience, life in the Spirit goes on. We may not always have optimum conditions for serving God, but we worship a God who can help us grow spiritually and live meaningfully in any situation.

CHAPTER SIX

TUMBLING EMOTIONS

What Do I Do When I Feel Overwhelmed and Helpless?

Rather than feel angry or depressed over what we have lost or will lose, we need to accept our feelings as appropriate reactions, understand why we have them, and use those feelings to motivate ourselves to harvest the riches of aging.[1]

Ellen McGrath, Ph.D., author of *When Feeling Bad Is Good*

One of my nieces works for a small private college in a small, scenic Midwestern town. When she told me she was thinking about applying for a job in a large city, I thought to myself, *If I were her I wouldn't move. I would love a situation like hers*.

I was walking on the campus of the high school near where I live when a teacher about my age exited the building. As I waved, I mumbled to myself, "She sure has it made—a good salary . . . competent and successful in her field. Must feel really good."

An attractive student bubbled with enthusiasm as she told me about several job possibilities she was considering when she graduated. As I smiled encouragingly, I thought, *I wish I had her options*.

When I read in a magazine about a Christian author with three book contracts on her desk, I threw the magazine across the room.

These pangs of jealousy didn't last long, but their sudden frequency puzzled me. By nature, I'm not a jealous person. Before midlife, I could count on one hand the times I had been jealous. Now fleeting feelings of jealousy started appearing frequently—jealousy of young women embarking on their careers, jealousy of successful people, jealousy of other writers, and jealousy of people whose lives appeared to be uncomplicated and easy.

Emotions—positive and negative—are part and parcel of being human. They add richness and texture to our lives, but they can also complicate them and interfere with growth. As one woman wrote, "Hearing from the Lord is difficult because of the fear of failure."

Lingering, unexpressed negative emotions can rob us of the eagerness to embrace life—that eagerness we had when we were younger. Instead, we become resigned to a lesser life and to aging rather than anticipating the possibilities of life's second half. We hesitate about making choices; we resist exploration and change.

Many of the women I surveyed talked about losses and the cumulative effect on their lives:

- "About the time I turned forty, I began feeling sad. It

came to me that my dreams were dying, and I was mourning their loss. The sadness has lingered and I think I will always have it with me."

- "I know it's been almost five years since my husband died, but sometimes it seems like only yesterday."
- "In the last several years there have been so many deaths of family and friends that I find myself anxious when the phone rings. My dad died five years ago and my mom is 72. Mom is in good health and is independent, but I still worry about her. My husband has had open-heart surgery and I worry about him."
- "I have experienced a number of losses or disappointments—relationships involving family members, body image, expectations for our children—that have tested my faith in God. What is He trying to teach me?"
- "My loneliness sometimes is overwhelming. Why, God, have You left me alone?"

Women also spoke of their fear of the unknown and how it holds them back.

- "I need to give complete control of my life to God. . . . I know in my head it needs to happen, but I fear loss of control."
- "I fear the future—aging, health, husband's health, money."
- "When I think about retirement, I have nothing positive to reflect on. It scares me."
- "I would like to do something meaningful, but education, financial security, and unfortunately, a lack of faith in God and myself keep me from doing this. It's a bit scary to step out on faith at this age."
- "I would like to go into private practice (nursing) and have my own business. What is keeping me from making this change is a feeling of insecurity—the unknown future. Starting over feels threatening to me."
- "I want to make a job change, but fear of the unknown, [the uncertainty of] benefits, money, and security keep me from making that change."

- "I would like a man in my life or to accept singleness to the point that it doesn't matter. Fear is keeping me from making this change."

These words contain some strong emotions, don't they? Fear paralyzes when left unexamined and unexpressed. So does anger, resentment, jealousy, sadness, grief, disappointment, depression, impatience, and loneliness—all emotions expressed by the women I surveyed when I asked them about the changes and challenges of their lives.

As you read about the losses and fears of other midlife women, do you recognize yourself? Are you feeling overwhelmed or helpless? Do you feel like there is nothing you can do? If so, it's just not true. Here are some things you can do.

EXPRESS YOUR EMOTIONS IN HEALTHY WAYS

Here are three healthy ways for releasing negative emotions: pray, talk with friends, seek professional help.

Pray honestly. Sometimes we hold our emotions inside instead of expressing them in prayer because we believe we can't really express to God how we feel; but the Bible shows us a number of honest pray-ers.

David admitted his impatience when he cried out, "How long must I wrestle with my thoughts and every day have sorrow in my heart?" (Psalm 13:2). On another occasion, David wanted to know why God had forsaken him (see Psalm 22:1). He described his distress as being in deep water with no foothold and said he had called until his throat was parched (see Psalm 69:1-4).

Moses expressed his frustration with God and the leadership task He had assigned him: "Oh, Lord, why have you brought trouble upon this people? Is this why you sent me?" (Exodus 5:22).

After Jeremiah incurred the wrath of the chief officer in the temple by following God's directions, Jeremiah confessed his anger and frustration over being God's spokesperson (see Jeremiah 20:7-18).

The night before His death, Jesus said to His disciples, "The sorrow in my heart is so great that it almost crushes me" (Matthew

26:38, TEV). He withdrew into the Garden of Gethsemane and repeatedly prayed for an escape: "My Father, if it is possible, may this cup be taken from me" (Matthew 26:39,42-44).

Praying honestly brings relief. It is prayer that rejuvenated David. Ever notice how his emotional prayers ended with praise? (See Psalm 13:5-6; 22:22-31; 69:30-36.)

God responded to Moses' frustration by promising to deliver the people (see Exodus 6:1-8).

As Jeremiah expressed his feelings, he realized he couldn't help but speak for God (see Jeremiah 20:9); and only by trusting and praising the Lord could he withstand the pressure and frustration of being a prophet (see verses 11-13).

Jesus left Gethsemane with renewed courage and strength. To His disciples He said, "Rise, let us go! Here comes my betrayer!" (Matthew 26:46).

When we pray honestly about the negative emotions we feel, we release those emotions, diffuse their power, and open the way for God to heal our hurtful feelings, renew our strength, and give us direction.

Talk with friends. Talking things out with a trusted friend or friends has good therapeutic value. Relief may come from verbally releasing what's bothering us, and once we get our feelings out in the open we may also gain insight as to why we feel the way we do. Our worries will likely appear more manageable. Talking paves the way for insight, positive action, and comforting support.

- "The death of my parents was particularly difficult. I was forty-two when my father died and forty-five when my mother died. It brought up many questions regarding my faith and beliefs. I found a great connection with other women who were and are going through the same thing."
- "In battling depression, I'm spending more time in God's Word and trying to pray more effectively. I've also turned to a couple of good Christian friends who are good listeners."

See a therapist. Some of us may need help with our emotions beyond what honest praying or talking with friends can give—we may need the help of a mental health professional. If you have never sought counseling before, the task of finding a therapist may seem daunting. Here's what Peggy, the counselor you first met in chapter 3, recommends:

Ask God to guide you to a therapist who can help you.

Ask friends, acquaintances, and church staff who they would recommend.

Call a counseling center and tell the receptionist the area in which you are looking for help (depression, anxiety, divorce recovery . . .). Tell her it is important for you to have a therapist with a Christian perspective. The receptionist will probably know of a therapist who will fit your qualifications and offer to make an appointment for you.

Attend the initial session expecting to meet a therapist you can work with, but also determine that you will seek another therapist if the first one makes you feel uncomfortable. If you do not feel "heard," valued, respected, and comfortable with this therapist, you will want to keep searching for the "right fit." An important part of emotional transformation takes places as a result of the warmth, support, and validation a woman receives from the therapist.

By the end of the first session, you should understand exactly how much each session will cost; by the end of the third session, the therapist should be able to give you a reasonable estimate of how many sessions you will need.

The results are worth the effort you may expend in finding a therapist who is right for you.

- "Through psychiatric help, including an antidepressant, I became the sane, happy person I used to be."
- "Participating actively in therapy and working on specific issues has allowed me to grow in so many ways."

TAKING ACTION

When we take action, we reduce our feelings of helplessness and gain some control over what happens. What actions we take will depend, of course, on what we are struggling with. Here are two examples of taking action.

1. Many of our fears and anxieties are money-related. We associate financial resources with a happy future. Twenty-six of the women who took my survey said that lack of money was keeping them from making positive changes. One woman said, "The lack of financial independence is the most frightening thing about growing old." What can we do?

We can *explore ways to earn more money* as Anita did. She wrote, "When I was fifty, I began selling vitamins and diet supplements. I never worked much outside the home after the first two years of married life. This has made me feel more independent."

We can *strengthen our job skills and/or learn new ones* that will give us more job flexibility. Look for reasonably priced continuing education classes at nearby colleges, check into courses at community colleges, or contact your local library about adult programs. Check with your boss about paying for training classes or your human resources director about in-house training.

We can *make changes in our spending and save money* for the future. When Harriet discovered that her husband's business was close to bankruptcy, she said, "I took over the books, put a curb on spending, and got rid of two incompetent employees. We sold our big house with its two mortgages and bought a condominium. If all goes well, we should be out of debt in five years."

We can *invest.* Nancy, the credit union vice president you met in chapter 4, wrote: "We outlive men, so we had better know what monies there are, how they got there, and how to make them grow."

Ultimate security, of course, lies in trusting God, but taking these other steps can reduce your worry and fear and give you more room to trust Him.

2. Another major worry or fear is that we will be lonely and forgotten in our later years. But if we invest continually in people, we will reap dividends later. My friend Les is a widow in her eighties and she has a bad back. I marvel at how many people help her out. One summer day when I was at her house, I noticed a new large oval flowerbed in her yard. With her back, I knew Les couldn't have pulled off such a project. I asked, "Who created your flower bed?"

Les said a dual-career couple about forty years younger than she was responsible. She said, "They take care of my yard, mowing and trimming it each week, and they planted the flower bed. They have been looking after my yard for years."

Les has story after story like this to tell. In fact, she confided,

"Sometimes people check on me so much that it infringes on my privacy!"

Les is a woman who invested—and who still invests—in people. I became friends with her because she invested in one of my sons. Her people investments are reaping valuable practical rewards at a time in her life when she can no longer care for herself as she once did. Though alone, her life is rich and full.

I'm not suggesting that you start viewing younger people in terms of what you can get out of them or that you have an attitude such as, "I'll do this for you, and you can help me out when I am old." What I am encouraging is a general willingness to invest in people. When we develop a lifestyle of investing in others, we give God resources to help meet our spiritual, emotional, and practical concerns as we age. Scripture tells us: "Give, and it will be given to you. A good measure, pressed down, shaken together and running over, will be poured into your lap. For with the measure you use, it will be measured to you" (Luke 6:38).

HARNESSING EMOTION'S POWER

In his book *The Seasons of a Woman's Life*, Daniel Levinson writes, "We must explore 'dimly lit' places in order to enter a new place that may in time be well lit."[2] We may not immediately understand why we feel the way we do. But in order to harness our emotions so they don't paralyze us, we need to identify them and understand their origins.

When I investigated why I was experiencing jealousy, as I mentioned at the beginning of this chapter, I found other emotions underneath the jealousy—sadness, resentment, disappointment, and particularly anger. As I traced the origins of these responses, it came back to one thing: dreams lying dormant and unfulfilled.

During my young adult years, I had expected to become one of God's spokeswomen—someone who delivered His messages, someone who encouraged and inspired others, and someone whose opinion counted. While I had done some of this—as many Christians do—I was not where I thought I should be. I was not a success, and this became painfully clear to me when I was asked to speak at a banquet for the honor graduates at an area high school. I wondered, *What could I tell them about success when I am a dabbler in many things and not successful in any?*

Each year I had a handful of speaking engagements and an occasional article published. I was an adjunct instructor at a small branch campus, with no opportunity of becoming a full-time college teacher. If something happened to my husband, I would not be able to support myself.

As I explored the "dimly lit areas of my heart," I saw that I had been in a holding position, as if I had been keeping a lid on my dreams. Many times they were put on the back burner in deference to someone else's needs. At other times, when I tried to pursue writing and speaking opportunities, doors closed more often than they opened.

Through it all, I was patient. I believed that if I were a "good girl," one day God was going to call me up to a place of success—just as the wedding host called up the guest who sat in the lowest place in Jesus' parable: "When you are invited, go and sit in the lowest place, so that your host will come to you and say, 'Come on up, my friend, to a better place.' This will bring you honor" (Luke 14:10, TEV). One day God would invite me up to a better place—translated, a place of success.

As fifty came and went, I realized that the "better place" hadn't happened and probably never would. I brooded about this for months until it occurred to me that I could use my anger to make my dreams come true. Instead of being the person in Jesus' parable who was admonished to take the lower seat, I would be the determined woman who pestered the unjust judge (see Luke 18:1-8) until she got justice. If others could do it, I could do it too.

To harness my anger and use its power, I wrote out ways I could be God's spokeswoman. I invited over a friend whom I suspected had a similar anger and had been waiting for God to act in her life. Over salad, I shared my list with her. This was to "nail down" my resolve.

In the upper left-hand corner of the list, I wrote, "We are called. No one is going to make the way open for us." In other words, if we were going to be the women God called us to be, it was up to us. No one was going to open the doors; we would have to open doors ourselves.

Some readers will question the appropriateness of using anger as a motivator. Admittedly, it's not the best approach, especially for believers. Ideally, we should begin with, "God, what do you want me to do?" But growth isn't always ideal or neat and orderly. If it hadn't been for discovering my anger and harnessing it, I don't know that I would have ever developed a vision for the person I could be in my middle years. Harnessing my anger changed a faint heart into a determined one.

Is Sin Part of the Problem?

After a spectacular victory at Jericho, Joshua relied on the strength of his army to defeat the small city of Ai. It wasn't enough. When they were driven back, a number of Israelites were killed. At that, "The hearts of the people melted . . ." (Joshua 7:5). Fear paralyzed them and they lost their desire to fight.

Overcome by their fear, they tore their clothing in agony of soul and prostrated themselves before the Lord. Joshua cried out to the Lord on behalf of the people. His prayer was full of questions and fear that they would all be killed (see Joshua 7:6-9).

Take note of God's response: "The Lord said to Joshua, 'Get up! Why are you lying on the ground like this? Israel has sinned!'" (Joshua 7:10-11, TEV). Ah, here was the explanation for the melting hearts. One of their group had broken God's command to destroy everything at the battle of Jericho except that which was reserved for the Lord's treasury. Their failure at Ai was the consequence of their sin, and it led to their fear.

Sin can contribute to our emotional struggles. If so, we need to repent and make corrections, just as the Israelites had to do (see Joshua 7:13-26).

One woman wrote, "The changes I have made since turning forty-five haven't been outward but have been more inward, stemming from a heartbreaking time when my daughter was rebellious. It caused me to do a lot of self-examination and I didn't like all I saw."

When we examine our feelings and our hearts, we may not like what we see, but it's important to look and make corrections. To not do so is to settle for faint hearts—hearts that will not have the courage to explore middlescent questions, entertain dreams, or embrace the future. I would rather have a strong, determined heart. How about you? What kind of heart do you want?

CHAPTER SEVEN

I'M MORE THAN MEETS THE EYE

Does Youthfulness Equal Attractiveness?

Please don't retouch my wrinkles.
It took me so long to earn them.[1]

Anna Magnani

AN ATTRACTIVE ANTIQUES DEALER IN HER EARLY FIFTIES TOLD ME, "I've always been considered attractive, and I think aging is harder for an attractive person than for one who has always been plain." Books like *New Passages* and *Unfinished Business* support her premise. But I disagree, and so do many other women. "In a society that reduces every woman to her appearance . . . it's a brave woman who bucks the system and insists she couldn't care less when age takes the bloom off the rose."[2] As one "plain woman" said, "I'm getting wrinkles and gray hair, and I hate it!"

Aging is so visible. As we notice the changes in our bodies, others are noticing too and may treat us differently. "Employers may unfairly dismiss us as incompetent and useless if we don't present a contemporary (translated 'youthful') image and deny us opportunities if we 'look our age' or have 'let ourselves go' by refusing to diet or dye our hair."[3]

Whether we are plain or attractive—or somewhere in between—we don't like getting wrinkles and losing muscle tone. The signs of aging get in the way of our dreaming about what to do with the rest of our lives because we're acutely aware of the link between appearance and success. I'll admit that I was disturbed about how my appearance might affect my chances to fulfill my dream to be God's spokeswoman.

In a different time or a different culture, we might not worry so much about the unattractiveness of aging. But we live in a culture that puts a premium on physical attractiveness and youthfulness. Advertisements and magazine headlines send us messages that we can and should do something about the telltale signs of aging: gray or thinning hair, wrinkles, loss of muscle tone. The message imprinted on our minds is that we aren't valuable unless we are attractive. This was something Catherine was keenly aware of when her long-distance relationship ended.

At that time, Catherine and I were attending the same church. I was involved in the lives of my children and in my writing; Catherine was single, a community activist, and a sports enthusiast. What drew us together for casual talk in the church hallways was that we were both new to the community. I was surprised one Sunday when she asked to talk with me in my home. By the tears that welled up in her eyes, I knew she didn't mean casual conversation.

In the quiet of my home, Catherine told me about a relationship that had begun before she moved. Since the move, she and Jeff had corresponded, talked on the phone every now and then, but seldom saw each other. Now he was proposing marriage.

That sounded like good news to me, so I said, "I don't understand, Catherine. What is the problem?"

"Oh, I can't marry him. He's boring; he has these eccentric habits that I could never live with. If I tell him no, though, that will be the end of our relationship."

I was still puzzled, so I probed further, "Would that be so bad? It isn't as if he were in your life every day and that you are going to miss him terribly. You have a full life with your career, your friends, and your church and community involvement."

In the quiet that followed, tears trickled down Catherine's cheeks. Finally she said, "I'm getting old," as if that explained everything, but it didn't. I was still puzzled, so Catherine pointed out her wrinkles and her thinning hair. Then I understood. Catherine had bought into our culture's message that the signs of aging made her less attractive. As long as there was a man in her life, even if he wasn't likable, it said to Catherine, "I am attractive. I am valued."

Danger Zone!

I'm not saying that it's wrong to want to look and feel our best—and to put some effort into it. Some advertised products will make a difference in our physical appearance. Many magazine articles offer valuable tips. Many of those tips involve good health practices or good grooming. Both can add to the quality of our life in the middle years, helping us to feel good and to be more confident. These are good things, and many women utilize them. However, with technologies available for changing biology and longevity, there's a danger of becoming preoccupied with our looks or maintaining a youthful appearance. This pursuit can limit who we can become and keeps us from fully enjoying our middle years.

Women who put all their efforts into maintaining their youthful appearance do so at the expense of cultivating other strengths that should come to the forefront during middle age. How will we recognize these strengths if we stay focused on our appearance? In our younger days, we may have resented how much women are judged by their outer appearance. Now is the time to let the world know that we are more than meets the eye.

Dr. Ellen McGrath, author of *When Feeling Bad Is Good,* writes, "The pressure to be physically perfect and remain forever young are two of the most consistent sources of depression among women."[4] Depression uses a great deal of emotional and spiritual energy that could be given over to enjoying our middle years.

Besides, trying to be physically perfect and to remain forever young are impossible standards to reach. No matter how much effort and money we put into appearing young, eventually the telltale signs of aging will appear.

How can we resist cultural pressure to focus on being attractive and instead be pleased with who we are? We may not be able to change our culture, but we can change how we respond to our culture.

WHO SAYS?

How we judge our attractiveness depends in part on how we internalize other people's perceptions and standards. During your young adult years, whose definition of beauty were you trying to live up to? Your mother's? Your husband's? Your friends'? The standards portrayed in magazines?

Nowhere is it written that we have to play by others' rules. You can write your own definition. You can pick a weight and a style you can live and be happy with. You can experiment with different colors, unconventional styles, and new ways of presenting yourself. As one survey respondent wrote, "When a woman nurtures her own style, it never goes out of date."

There are many ways to be attractive. In *Getting Over Getting Older*, Letty Cottin Pogrebin writes about studying ordinary midlife women who seem to attract people easily. She said,

"The most enchanting of them share certain traits: they radiate self-confidence without egoism, feel passionate about something, show a lively interest in other people and in the world around them, and communicate their personality through their eyes, smile, speech, passion, and also their 'plumage.'"[5] By "plumage," Pogrebin means the self-decoration that helps women convey who they are. It may be wearing hats, bright colors, or a certain kind of earrings—something that says, "This is me!"

How You See

Our eyes are constantly moving, evaluating, and taking in observations. When Eve "saw" that the forbidden fruit "was good for food and pleasing to the eye, and also desirable for gaining wisdom, she took some and ate it" (Genesis 3:6). Like Eve, we "see" more than just the objects in front of us.

With our eyes, we internalize other people's perceptions of us. We compare ourselves with others and develop an image of how we *ought* to look. But we can change this image by changing how we "see," as Evy did. When Evy was diagnosed with amyotrophic lateral sclerosis (ALS, or Lou Gehrig's disease), her neurologist said, "Evy, you have six to twelve months to live. . . . "[6]

Before she died, Evy wanted to discover what unconditional love was. To make this discovery, Evy knew that she would have to first accept her own body, which she had always hated. As Evy describes it, "There I sat in front of a mirror in my wheelchair . . . my once firm, strong muscles had wasted away into flaccid, useless ones. . . . I looked with disgust at my deteriorating body."

Sitting alone day after day, she began analyzing her thoughts. She said, "I noticed . . . a relentless obsession with weight. I was sure that if I became 'skinny' enough, an admirable body would magically greet me in the mirror. And now I sat in a wheelchair with acutely atrophying muscles."

Evy began to write down the many thoughts, both negative and positive, she had about her body in the course of a day. When she saw the huge amount of negative thoughts on paper, she said, "I was forced to confront the degree of hatred I had for my body."

To counter this ingrained negativity, every day Evy singled out one aspect of her body that was acceptable to her, no matter how small. Next, she used that item to challenge the negativity. After every negative thought, she wrote a positive statement such as "My hair is truly pretty," or "I have lovely hands," or "My bright eyes and warm smile light up my face." Each day she added a new positive item as the rewriting continued.

One day she noticed that she had no negative thoughts about her body. She said, "I could look in the mirror at my naked reflection and honestly be awed by its beauty. I was totally at peace, with a complete, unalterable acceptance of the way my body was."

Accepting her body brought about unexpected and unsolicited physical improvements. Her physical body stopped deteriorating. "But," Evy says, "if the outcome had been different . . . , it would not have altered or diminished the inherent beauty I now accepted."[7]

Since Evy changed the way she "sees" her body, she joyously awakes each day, filled with enthusiasm for life. The same result will ensue when we change the way *we* view our aging bodies.

BADGES OF HONOR

When my son Ben was nine years old, he had a go-cart accident. He intended to brake, but instead he hit the accelerator and drove into a barbed wire fence. The wire tore open his chest and, after the stitches, he was left with several ugly scars. Ben never wanted anyone to see his scars. When he went swimming, he always wore an oversized white T-shirt. When his older brother, Jim, found out, he said in a perfect Tim Allen imitation, "Get that shirt off. Those are your battle scars. Shows you're a man." That was the last we saw of the T-shirt.

I thought of Jim's words the night I heard a television anchor say, "Queen Elizabeth experienced another tragedy today. Her official portrait was released and it showed all of the wrinkles of her seventy-one years." I bristled. *Well, why not? She's earned every one of her wrinkles. Why should they be regarded as a tragedy? Could they not be badges of honor?*

Wrinkles show that we are women who have lived. Age spots say we've been around awhile; we've experienced life. Our age and our "experience entitle us to wear our graying hair, wrinkles, or extra pounds—badges of mature womanliness—with pride."[8] The Bible says, "Gray hair is a crown of splendor; it is attained by a righteous life" (Proverbs 16:31).

One woman told me, "I much admire a woman over forty-five who is self-confident, who is not intimidated by her gray hair or a few wrinkles, and who is not constantly trying to be her 'younger self,'" and I agree. If we cultivate our warmth and curiosity, our ease in relating to people, our intelligence and imagination, our wit and wisdom, we will not be so preoccupied and self-conscious with how people see us. If we enter a room with curiosity and a twinkle in our eye, expecting to meet somebody who will be interested in what we have to say, and expecting to be interested in what others have to say, we will be attractive. People will be drawn to us.

A striking fact stands out in Scripture: The majority of biblical women aren't described by their physical appearance. We aren't told, for example, what Ruth looked like, though many of us picture her as pretty. We also don't know how Jesus' mother, Mary, appeared. While a few Old Testament women such as Esther are described as beautiful, the New Testament contains no reference to women's physical attractiveness.

A godly woman's worth isn't measured by the beauty of her face, the shape of her body, the style of her hair, the brand of her cosmetics, or the fit of her clothing. The Bible stresses that a woman's inner qualities, her personal relationships, and her love for the Lord are more important than her appearance.

> Charm is deceptive, and beauty is fleeting; but a woman who fears the LORD is to be praised. (Proverbs 31:30)

> It is not fancy hair, gold jewelry, or fine clothes that should make you beautiful. No, your beauty should come from within you—the beauty of a gentle and quiet spirit that will never be destroyed and is very precious to God. (1 Peter 3:3-4, NCV)

In the Sermon on the Mount, Jesus said, "You are the light of the world" (Matthew 5:14). He did not say, "You have to be physically attractive in order to gain light." He said, "You are light." Take that thought with you as you go to the mall or when you pay your bills. As you interact with people, respond to them as if you are God's light. As you go to work and deal with difficult coworkers, act as if you are light. As you rub your body with lotion before you go to bed, thank God for every inch of it. Remind yourself that He created you and that He created you to age. With the body and mind He has given you, you have everything you need to be a light to the world.

We have lived through adolescence not yet knowing who we are, and young adulthood trying to please others, putting on our masks, and never feeling we could truly be ourselves. Middlescence is our opportunity for dreaming, for discovering who we really are, and for being delighted with what we discover. Once we begin to accept and enjoy the roundness of middle age, the wrinkles and sags that come naturally with maturing, we are free to devote our energies to the exciting adventures God has for us. It's not a matter of the culture being convinced that we have lots to offer the world; the question for each of us is, *Am I convinced?*

CHAPTER EIGHT

CRINGING AT THE THOUGHT

Help! Am I on My Way to Being Obsolete?

If you see a 90-year-old man mowing his own grass, you say, "Isn't he wonderful?" Is the bedridden older person less wonderful? Our attitudes reflect the pervasive stereotype that older people are useless. Therefore, if they can do anything at all, we say they are wonderful.[1]

Dr. Carol Pierskalla,
answering a question about attitudes on aging

DRESSED IN YOUR POWER SUIT, YOU SIT AT A TABLE BY YOURself in the company lunchroom. You choose to eat alone because you are trying to finish a report. But the laughter of the group of young women at the next table distracts you. Without looking up, you overhear them talking about the oldest woman in your department. One of them says, "She doesn't have a clue about what is happening. When is this company going to get rid of her?" You cringe at the thought of anyone ever making a statement like that about you.

You've been one of several Bible study leaders in your church's women's ministries program for five years—a position you took when your last child left home. You did it to "help out" but discovered that you thrived. With plenty of time to devote to God's Word, your life centered around your preparation. You were visibly shaken when the women's ministry director discussed with the Bible study leaders how to involve younger women. A leader in her mid-thirties said, "I think we need younger Bible study leaders. Some women I know aren't coming because the study seems stuffy and unrelated to their lives." You wonder, *Could they mean me? Do they think I'm too old to teach the Bible to younger women?*

The director of your church's outreach department keeps asking you to play the piano for services at a local nursing home. You have found yourself avoiding him because you've run out of reasonable excuses. What you can't tell him is that you don't want to go. You avoid nursing homes because you don't want to be reminded of what could happen to you someday—that you could end up old, discarded, and forgotten. Like the psalmist, you pray, "Do not cast me away when I am old." (Psalm 71:9)

Do any of these scenarios sound familiar? They sure do to me. In my attic is a portable manual typewriter. Early in my writing career, I used it to produce decent-looking manuscripts. It fit snugly in a small suitcase so I could take it wherever I wanted. I never had to worry about finding an electrical outlet. All in all, it was a dependable machine, and it still works. But if I put an ad in the newspaper to sell it, no one would respond. In this age of word processing and laser printers, no one wants a manual typewriter. The machine is obsolete.

I've feared being just like that typewriter: old, discarded, out of style, no longer useful or valued. Oh, we don't talk about it in the same way we talk about hormone replacement therapy or weight gain, but it hovers in the background. It's no wonder many midlife women feel this way, given our fast-paced technological culture.

Where Does This Fear Come From?

Cultural values. Athalene readily admits to being afraid of becoming old, lonely, and unwanted. She says, "I fear I will get to a point in life when I no longer have meaningful work to do. I feel that way because society places such a high value on youth and productivity."[2]

Our culture puts a premium on youth and productivity, and that's one reason why Ben's leaving home bothered me. As long as I had a child at home, I had a connection with youth that I believed would help keep my students interested in what I had to say. I could remain productive.

Ever-changing technology. My friend Sandy, a promotional writer who works out of her home, is constantly upgrading her computer and software. She said, "I try to keep up but it seems that my frustration level peaks every time I have to start using a new software program. Nothing ever seems to install right and I have no way of fixing it myself."

I can relate. I've tried ignoring technology, and I've tried plunging in and using it. When I ignored technological advances, I felt out of it; I felt that the world was moving on and leaving me behind. When I get new software, the hard-to-comprehend manuals make me feel inferior. *What's wrong with me that I can't figure this out?*

Competition of younger adults. Arlene, who is in her fifties, says, "I wonder what it will be like if I am still operating my public relations business when I'm sixty-five. I'll be competing at book-selling conventions with twenty- and thirty-year-old publicists! Imagine!"

Women who don't have to support themselves in a competitive job situation might not identify with Arlene's concerns, but if they have to start looking for a job, they will. They'll wonder, *At my age, how can I compete? Who will want to hire me?*

A friend of mine was fifty-one when her company was bought out and she was let go. She wanted to change careers but was finding it difficult. She said, "I didn't know life could be this tough. Employers can't believe you can learn a new job, that you can make the transition, and that you will work at this age for what they pay."

Our observations. In our younger days—and even now—we took in, interpreted, and stored observations about people in their late forties, fifties, and early sixties. For example, how did you view your parents when they were your age? A woman in one of my discussion groups said, "I didn't think my parents had a life at fifty. And now, at fifty, my children are thinking the same thing about me."

Through the years we have taken note of how some older people are treated, and we fear being treated the same way. One woman noted: "I've watched other old people—even some where I work—who are 'out of it.' Not senile by any means, but just not culturally aware. The world speeded up as they were slowing down, and now we humor them . . . and we try to protect them from making disastrous or just inefficient decisions, which they do frequently anyway. It's scary to think of becoming like that."

I don't know if all women fear becoming obsolete, but I do know this: If we see ourselves as obsolete, we will conclude that life is over and we won't entertain dreams about who we can be and what we can do. The fear is tenacious, so we have to fight it. Here are some ways do just that.

STARVE THE FEAR

All of us have fears. What we don't want to do is feed our fear, helping it along with what we say or think.

How frequently do you blame any forgotten name or detail on

"I must be getting old"? I've noticed, though, that none of my young students blame their memory losses on getting old, and they forget plenty! Other things besides failing memories cause us to forget: stress, poor listening habits, lack of focus, for example. When you forget something, instead of saying "I must be getting old," say "I have so many things going"—inner interpretation: I'm so productive—"I can't keep up with all the details."

Another way we feed fear is by overgeneralizing and making long-term predictions of the future. When I asked Joanie if she was afraid of being obsolete, she said, "Well, sure. All the time. Without regular employment and with multiple surgeries for several years, I've often thought: *Is this what I have to look forward to? Rapidly becoming nobody, and not feeling very good either?* What does one do for comfort when there really is nothing left to look forward to—when the friends and family are distant or dead, when the body is inefficient, when the next major transition is over the Jordan?"

Did you notice how Joanie's fear escalated from "surgeries" to "nothing to look forward to" to "becoming nobody" to death? How much better if she could counter her fear with, "I am temporarily sidetracked with surgeries. When this is over and my body has healed, I will look for a job."

When Ben left home and I was afraid my students would no longer be interested in what I had to say, I fought my fear by compiling contrary evidence. This is the process I followed.[3]

- *Fact*: Had one student ever checked me out before taking my class? "Mrs. Poinsett, do you have any children living at home? If you do, I want to take your class. If you don't, I will seek another instructor." No, not one student had ever asked if I had children at home.
- *Fact:* Weren't there teachers older than me who were doing an effective job of teaching? Yes, there were. Students enrolled in their classes.
- *Fact*: Had I ever refused to learn from someone who was old? No, older people are full of wisdom, and I have learned much from them.
- *Fact*: Wouldn't God be with me in the next stage of my life? Doesn't God always have significant work for a

> person to do at any age? Doesn't the Bible say, "Even to your old age and gray hairs I am he, I am he who will sustain you?" (Isaiah 46:4)

The facts prompted me to pray, "Father, help me move ahead into the next stage in life. Help me believe I will still have significance as a person and as a teacher." My fears over my students considering me obsolete dissipated. Now I wonder how I could ever have been so irrational, but that is what fear will do to your thinking.

ACTING "AS IF"

If a woman has embraced society's values on youthfulness, she may blame what is wrong with her life on her aging physical appearance. She may tell herself:

- If I looked younger, I could get a better job.
- If I were prettier, I could attract a man who would marry me.
- If I were more attractive, I could be a mentor to younger women.

Dr. Joyce Brothers writes, "In ninety-nine cases out of a hundred, the person who believes her looks are blocking her from the life she wants is wrong."[4] Did you catch that? Ninety-nine women out of one hundred are wrong about their looks keeping them from the life they want!

Instead of "if-ing," ask yourself, *How would I respond if I were younger? How would I handle the job interview? How would I handle social situations?* Take your answer and then proceed to act that way. "Acting as if" is a solid psychological principle. If we act *as if* we are productive and attractive, we'll feel that way—and that's how people will most likely see us.

ENGAGE YOUR MIND

One woman I surveyed said she admired women who were "constantly looking for and enjoying new learning experiences. This seems to stave off the tendency to allow the aging process to stagnate one's life, thus making one 'old.' Once a person gives into that process, all power to be effective and vibrant is gone."

She's right. An engaged mind is an occupied mind; it doesn't have room for fear. A focused mind keeps us from being afraid and gives us confidence. We may occupy our minds in order to stay sharp and competitive, or we may do it simply because we are interested in learning. In *New Passages,* Gail Sheehy reports that she found a desire to go back to school to be an almost universal yearning among women in middle life.[5]

When we are committed to active learning—whether through books, classes or seminars, or personal Bible study—our intelligence increases. "New learning exceeds the rate at which we forget. The research on lifespan development of human abilities shows that people who have compelling interests and activities and remain socially connected actually increase their IQ scores as they age."[6] It is only when we withdraw, when what goes out exceeds what comes in, that intelligence declines.[7]

Faye, the director of a child development center, is well aware of this research, and it's making a difference in how she plans for the future. She said, "I believe that preventive measures taken when I'm younger will benefit me in later years. I am developing plans for after retirement. I want to write children's books and volunteer at various organizations. I am developing new skills now and networking with individuals who have knowledge in these areas. I want to have a plan for staying busy and involved with other projects after I retire." Her dreams engage her mind and quell her fear of being obsolete.

Be an Expert

Even those of us who see ourselves as generalists are going to arrive at age forty-five or fifty with a backlog of information or skills. You can choose to keep growing by studying, researching, and/or improving in areas like these, thereby becoming an expert:

- Family historian
- Church historian
- Family social expert
- Professional specialist
- A biblical sage

Being an expert will contribute to our self-confidence and ensure that people will seek us out, canceling the possibility of feeling like we're of no use to anyone.

WHAT'S NEVER OBSOLETE

There's always room in this world for people who love, who are compassionate and kind, who show interest in others and are good listeners.

I've always believed this, but as I wrote it here, I was prompted to think about why I've been more concerned about being accomplished and successful than being compassionate and kind. Could it be because the world doesn't recognize and applaud spiritual strengths? Had society's values become important in my life without my having realized it? Had I, too, bought the message that only if we are young, productive, and attractive we will be valued?

Athalene, mentioned previously, shares my concern. "I think my perspective gets out of focus in at least two ways: (1) I focus on the world's definition of importance, and (2) I focus on the many distractions that get in the way of finding God's 'agenda' for me."[8]

Perhaps for some of us, fighting the fear of being obsolete means getting back to the basics: "Don't let the world around you squeeze you into its own mold, but let God remake you so that your whole attitude of mind is changed. Thus you will prove that the will of God is good, acceptable to him and perfect" (Romans 12:2, PH).

The director of our student Christian organization in college was always quoting Romans 12:2. She was concerned that our young minds would be molded by the world's standards. (From what I've learned of middlescence, we are in danger of the same thing.) She encouraged us to find God's will for our lives. She said, "You can fight the world's influence when you are sure of who you are—that you are being God's person and living out His call."

That's one reason why our quest to answer the question *What will I do with the rest of my life?* is so important. When we are confident of God's call—when we know who we are and how valuable we are to Him—we won't fear being obsolete. God always has meaningful work for us to do. Spiritual strengths never go out of style.

PART TWO

COME, DREAM WITH ME

CHAPTER NINE

THE EMERGING POWER WOMAN

What Do I Have Going for Me?

The age of fifty is the beginning of a new kind of freedom. . . . You've reached a measure of success in your work, you've made most of your big mistakes—the kind that bring you trouble which you could have avoided by the mere use of better judgment. You know a little something about yourself—what you're really like, what you want from life, what you mean to give back to life. . . . Oh, Genie, this time of life is it—from now on, this is it.[1]

George Barry, in his seventies,
to Eugenia Price when she turned fifty

Once a vision began forming in my mind of who I could be and what I could do, my heart cried, "Ah, yes! There *is* life after forty-five." But it took awhile for me to get there. Not only did I have to identify and face what was holding me back in order to let those things go, I also had to build a future for myself. I had to dream again of who I could be.

When I initially contemplated the rest of my life, I didn't like any of the pictures that came to mind. The landscape was always gray and bleak; the woman in them was powerless. All I could see before me was a settled life, possibly a stagnant one where growth ceased. I don't know how long I would have retained these negative images if some items in my library research hadn't grabbed my attention and helped me see myself in new ways. In this chapter I'd like to share with you some of the things that started me dreaming again, ideas that excited and motivated me about who I could become and how God might use me.

Power Surge

David Gutmann, a developmental and clinical psychologist, collected data on the psychological growth and patterns of change in older women. Several patterns suggested that, across a wide range of societies, the older woman moves aggressively toward a position of matriarchy and the assumption of power. Gutmann argued that the virility of the older woman is released when she emerges from the adult period of chronic emergency (otherwise known as parenting!).[2]

Anthropologist Margaret Mead noted a tremendous release of energy that becomes available to women after menopause. She called it PMZ for postmenopausal zest.[3]

In the physiological metamorphosis of menopause, the ratio of estrogen to testosterone decreases markedly. The ratio of testosterone to estrogen in a postmenopausal woman may be up to twenty times higher than in a woman who is still ovulating and making estrogen in her ovaries.[4] Dr. Joan Borysenko, in *A Woman's Book of Life,* connects this rise in testosterone to the development of the passion and confidence that can encourage postmenopausal women to stand up for what they think is right and to be a conduit of wisdom.[5] Gail Sheehy connects it to a resurgence of adventurousness, independence, and assertiveness in women.[6]

Colette Dowling called her book for women turning fifty *Red Hot Mamas*. Early in her research, she heard about support groups with this name popping up in California for women this age. While the term "includes sexuality, it is not merely sexual. It has to do with the integrity, aggressiveness, and self-affirmation of women who are able, at midlife, to respect themselves."[7]

In her book *Our Health, Our Lives,* Dr. Eileen Hoffman says that most of her midlife patients feel freed up and energized. "For these women, menopause marks a time of life when the sense of self is stronger than ever, accomplishments are many, and personal power is at its peak."[8]

Most of these observations are just that, observations, so they cannot serve as building blocks for developing conclusive statements about *all* middlescent women. But they can be blocks for building a foundation for dreams, helping us to recognize our potential. As I noted the strengths they mentioned, my eyes opened to possibilities.

- Virility
- Zest
- Passion
- Confidence
- Wisdom
- Spirit of adventure
- Independence
- Assertiveness
- Integrity
- Aggressiveness
- Self-affirmation
- Freed up
- Energized
- Strong sense of self

When I added these up, my reaction was, *Sounds like power to me.* Indeed, a unifying theme tied the unrelated items together: Each identified a release of energy or vitality, as if a power surge was taking place. Did this explain what was pressing against my rib cage? Was there a burst of energy inside me waiting to be set free?

My curiosity was aroused and I wondered if middle-aged women would make similar observations. To find out, I asked them, What do you enjoy most about your present age? What kinds of power do you observe and admire in women over forty-five?

Although their answers were broad and varied, certain strengths popped up again and again, and they were very similar to the list mentioned above.

FREEDOM

Cries of freedom rang throughout many of the women's responses, so much so that visions of freed slaves danced in my head. I could hear them singing, "Free at last, free at last, thank God almighty, we're free at last."[9]

While it's not true for every mother, midlife typically means an empty nest. With all the talk about the empty nest syndrome, I was surprised that so many women sang the joys of being free from childbearing, child caring, and child rearing. They talked of being free from:

- The constancy of around-the-clock, day-in and day-out responsibilities
- Too much to do and not enough time to do it
- The endless financial needs associated with rearing children
- Having to wear too many hats, fill too many roles
- Conflicting schedules
- Always having to think of the children first
- The pressures of rearing well-behaved, talented children

But freedom's chorus had other verses that sang of less competition and strife.

Young adulthood, beginning in our late twenties and ending in our middle forties, is about establishing our niche in the workplace, our community, our family, and our church. Under reasonably favorable conditions, the rewards of this stage are enormous, but the costs often equal or exceed the benefits. The effort involved can be intense and unrelenting.

Tuned in to the opinions of others, we may try so hard to impress that we Jell-O-mold ourselves into what we believe others want because we want to be respected and successful. We evaluate our success by constantly comparing ourselves to others.

At midlife, the pressure to compete with others may subside. Avery, divorced and with no children, summarized what many survey respondents alluded to: "When I turned forty there was an immediate dropping off of the sense that I am competing with other women."

Cecelia, a single woman in her forties who has returned to school to get a degree, wrote, "I enjoy that I am past the age of worrying about what everyone thinks about me. I would not want to do anything to upset someone on purpose, but I have other things to worry about than trying to impress everyone in one way or another."

Another woman said, "My goals are changing; I am no longer so eager to please or so willing to allow my sense of well-being to be determined by how others evaluate me."

In young adulthood, most of us focused on acquiring possessions. We incurred heavy financial obligations when our earning power was still relatively low. What we and/or our husbands earned always had to be stretched in too many ways. By the time we are past forty-five—or our children have finished college—financial burdens may be easing. As one respondent expressed it, "I have the freedom to go where and when I want. I am no longer confined by lack of a baby-sitter or lack of funds."

Wisdom

While a person can be wise at any age, a deep well of wisdom can come from living. Many of the women I surveyed talked of having learned valuable lessons about life and living, and knowing so much more about how the world works than they knew when they were younger. They know what's important and what isn't worth their energy. They have a better understanding of human nature and can make sense of what they see and hear. Here are some of the things they said, in their own words.

- "Women over forty-five have greater emphasis and concern for the really important issues of life."
- "I admire women who have the wisdom to realize that life requires choices and that it is important to enjoy what advantages one has."
- "Wise women focus more on a bigger picture than when [they] were younger."
- "They have the ability to see to the heart of the matter."
- "Women over forty-five have gained the wisdom to know that a person's heart, mind, and emotions are infinitely more important than what she looks like or how successful she is or who she knows."

As I read these comments, I couldn't help but think of how the Bible encourages the pursuit of wisdom: "Believe in the value of wisdom, and it will make you great. Use it, and it will bring honor to you. Like flowers in your hair, it will beautify your life. Like a crown, it will make you look beautiful" (Proverbs 4:8-9, NCV).

Sense of Self

The word "self" peppered the women's descriptions of the power they observed, admired, and experienced: self-confident, self-assured, self-aware, self-sufficient, and self-directed. They talked of coming home to themselves and being delighted with what they found.

- "I've finally 'come of age.' I can state my opinion and have it acknowledged by others—including men—as valid."
- "I don't feel the need to impress people any longer; I can just be myself."
- "I feel 'at home' with myself."
- "I'm grown up, finally."
- "I feel like I've arrived. I'm secure and satisfied with

who I am and what I am doing."

- "I am growing into more of an awareness of who I am as God made me."
- "I *can* think for myself, I found. I *can* make decisions without needing permission or affirmation from others before coming to my own conclusions."

To a woman who has always had a strong sense of self, this kind of self-discovery in midlife may be perplexing. But for many of us, our young adult years were the "proving" years. We were proving to our parents that we could be responsible adults. Simultaneously, many of us were heavily involved in parenting—proving to the world that we could do it right. If we were married, we tried to please our husbands because we wanted a good marriage. We worked at being Christians who would have a strong witness and be a good example to others. We aimed for success, learned job skills, and built careers. Whew! With so much "proving" going on, a woman may not have been aware she had a self!

After playing for years to her audiences—her family, her coworkers, her fellow Christians—a woman may have felt she was *their* person. In midlife, many women finally feel free to ask, What do *I* want? What is important to *me?* What are *my* dreams?

Independence

One woman who took my survey observed, "Women over forty-five are not scared kids anymore." Another said that women over forty-five have more chutzpah than when they were younger. More than one woman noted that this is especially true of women in their fifties and sixties. "There is a sense of 'what have I got to lose?' or 'I'm not getting any younger. If I'm going to do what I want to do, I might as well do it now.'"

Being independent serves us well.

- It helps us fight the social bias in our culture that stigmatizes individuals on the basis of age.
- It gives us the spunk to resist the scripts that have been written for us.

- It gives us the courage to define who we are going to be and how we are going to live.
- It helps us eliminate activities/responsibilities from our lives that are no longer meaningful.
- It gives us a spirit of adventure, which we will need when we want to commit ourselves to new avenues and experiences.
- It helps us to be women of integrity, to openly declare what we believe to be true and right and good, even when there are risks.

Being independent does not mean we throw caution to the wind or that we become less spiritual or caring. Actually what women said they admire is "independence *and* __________." For example:

- "I admire a woman who has found a balance between a loving relationship with her spouse and yet is independent enough to manage if she has to."
- "I admire women who are independent and yet yielded to the Lord and to His authority."
- "I admire women who are independent in most areas of their lives yet have a true concern for others."
- "I admire women who have the ability to become financially independent but choose to spend their time and energy pursuing higher goals."
- "I admire women who can be wives and still have their own identity—who are not so completely identified as someone's wife, mother, and so on, but also identified as a person in her own right."

Being independent does not mean we don't care about people or that we no longer need them. Just the opposite is true; people continue to be very important to most women in midlife.

Deeper Relationships

One woman said, "The finest and purest friendships often develop after age forty-five." Many women who emerge from middlescence appear to be both willing and able to take advantage of opportunities for more satisfactory close relationships. When you are free to be yourself, you are free to enjoy your relationships.

The women I surveyed enthusiastically noted these relationship pluses for this time of life.

- Quality time with spouse
- Enjoying and influencing grandchildren
- Enjoying the changed relationship with children
- Mentoring and investing in young adults
- Quality time with old friends
- Time to develop and to cultivate new friendships

A woman who combines wisdom with her strong interest in people, a strong sense of self, and independence is naturally suited for:

- Strong matriarchal roles in the family
- Leadership/mentoring positions in the church and community
- Formal and informal counseling
- Management opportunities in the workplace

As I read about the strengths these women identified in their own lives and in other women they know, my mental pictures of the woman over forty-five began changing. That gray, bleak landscape turned into living color. The woman in the center was no longer powerless; she was strong, wise, independent, and caring.

Colette Dowling said that whenever she mentioned the term "red hot mamas" in her lectures, women cheered.[10] That's what I wanted to do once I realized the potential for midlife women. I even developed my own affectionate term for the middlescent woman coming into her own: the emerging power woman. I like that term. It excites me. It makes me feel that I can do and be.

Of course, these traits as given by the respondents are not automatic. Not all women over forty-five will have these traits, and some women won't want them. But the fact that these traits were recognized in many women over forty-five raised my consciousness about the possibility of their being present in my life. And that's what we need: possibility thinking. The realm of possibility is where we dream and begin building our plans for the future. What we each need to answer is, *What is my potential? What do I have going for me?*

Potential Recognition

Looking at the traits already mentioned here is one way to begin thinking about our potential. We can use these traits as a benchmark to evaluate our strengths.

- Do I feel free? If not, why not? What is holding me back?
- Am I a woman of wisdom? How am I wise?
- Do I have a strong sense of self or a weak sense of self?
- Are there unexplored areas of my life?
- Am I more independent or dependent?
- Are my relationships what I would like them to be?

If you want to build a foundation for the future, make a list of your personal strengths. They may be totally different from those mentioned here. Whether or not you identify with any of the traits mentioned in this chapter, you have strength that can be mined and developed. Be reflective and prayerful about this, doing it as an exercise over several weeks.

Ask others how they see you. When I asked my discussion group to be prepared to tell us about their strongest attributes, I thought I would ask my husband what mine were. Over dinner, I asked him how he would describe my strengths. Without hesitating, he said, "You are a woman of conviction and it is important to you that you express those convictions; you are a people-pleaser and you have a genuine concern for people." Bingo! Right on target.

The people who know us make observations about us, and those observations can be a big help when we're trying to evaluate our potential. Bob's words helped me see why power was important to me and yet they were also a stark reminder that I needed to become less of a people-pleaser. Expressing convictions and pleasing people aren't always compatible.

As we appraise our potential, we need to remind ourselves that we all have one thing going for us: the freedom to choose. We are on the threshold of the second half of our life. What are we going to do? Are we going to seek new directions, take advantage of opportunities, and create new roles that fit our expanded energies and strengths? The choice is up to us, and many women are choosing to make change. Among the survey respondents, 125 out of 169 women said they had made positive changes in their lives since turning forty-five. They have learned new skills, returned to school, plunged into new careers, rediscovered their creativity, and embarked on new adventures.

We are free to make decisions about our future. We are free to dream.

God's Power and Our Power

I'll admit that not everyone shared my enthusiasm for the concept of power. Some women are uncomfortable talking about power. Power to them has a negative aroma; they associate it with aggression and dominance. As one woman responded, "Not many of my friends would actually seek 'power'—having given up the power goal when they left the workplace. It most certainly is not my motivation; I am primarily seeking opportunities to serve—with compassion. I have *no* need to be in charge at all! My comfort zone is found in contributing, not in power seeking."

A dictionary definition of "power" is the "ability to do and the capacity to act effectively." Power does not have to be loud or abrasive to be effective. Power can be wielded in various ways. Women in management believe in the power of personality. They lead by charisma, sharing power, and including others in decision making. They motivate not by intimidation but by building self-respect.

Some Christian women resist thinking about having power because they insist we should only think in terms of God's power, not our own. But both are important. When we recognize our special strengths, we give God more channels for Him to use. The horizon of what God can do with and through us broadens. This is why becoming aware of strengths is so important.

God has special blessings or gifts for us at every age. Part of the growth work in middlescence is becoming more aware of our gifts. We then have a choice: Will we give those gifts to God for Him to use? We can let His power work in and through our particular gifts, or we can go it alone. We can use our liberated energy and our wisdom to make this world a better place, or we can use the gifts simply to further our own interests.

It is not God's power *or* our power. It is God's power *and* our power.

As Athalene put it, "To me, a powerful woman has control and say-so in her life. She is an active person, not reactive. As a Christian, I think a powerful woman refuses to let her womanhood become an excuse for inactivity or exercising little control of her own life. She chooses to let her relationship with God empower her for whatever role she is given."[11]

None of us see power in the same way. But what is important is that we do not see ourselves as *powerless*. We have the capacity to do and to act. Consequently, we have choices to make.

- Will we open ourselves to new and more meaningful ways to be alive?
- Will we open ourselves to new avenues and experiences?
- Will we acknowledge our gifts and surrender them to God?

CHAPTER TEN

TICK-TOCK, TICK-TOCK

I Feel Rushed. . . . Do I Have Time to Dream?

Seventy years is all we have—eighty years, if we are strong. . . . Teach us how short our life is, so that we may become wise.[1]

Psalm 90:10,12(TEV)

BERNICE NEUGARTEN, A GERONTOLOGY SPECIALIST, ONCE SAID that when we are young we count our ages by how long it has been since birth. A time comes, however, when we also begin to contemplate how long we have left to live. When we begin to use both the time since birth and the time we have left, we've reached middle age.[2]

Many midlife women have more time to pursue more things, as we mentioned in chapter 9. But just as our time is freed up, we are also becoming aware of how little time we have left. This realization may occur on a birthday. When the smoke rises from so many lighted candles on our cake, reality hits. Or it may occur when we start having health problems or someone close to us dies. As Paula said, "When my mother died, I became keenly aware of my own mortality. . . . So I want to cram as much into life as I can with the time I have left!"

Time also seems to be going by much faster. "We glide along the tides of time as swiftly as a racing river" (Psalm 90:6, TLB). We may feel rushed with a now-or-never kind of feeling or have a heightened awareness of the brevity of life. As one woman said, "Now that I am forty-six years old I feel my life on earth is half over, and there is so much I want to do for the Lord and so little time to do it in." Some of us feel that if we don't hurry, it will be too late to do the things we want to do. A panicky feeling lodges in our throats and an inner voice warns, "Hurry! You don't have forever."

Our outlook may become dismal; Paula described it as "depressing." We may grieve over missed opportunities or the shortness of life. When these feelings come, it's important to acknowledge and embrace them so that we can come to terms with our mortality. Odd as it may sound, if we want to make good use of the time we have left on this earth, we must first accept the inevitable.

ACCEPTING THE INEVITABLE

If a true-or-false question read, "Every person will die," we would answer, "True," and yet we go through most of our life denying it. Dr. Rachel Naomi Remen writes, "The denial of death is the most common way we all edit life."[3] But at midlife we can't deny it any longer. As the tick-tock of life's clock picks up speed, the true and false question loses its objectivity. "Unpredictably, in the midst of a party, on a beautiful summer afternoon, when your daughter and son-in-law are showing you photographs of their vacation, while you are listening to music, or riding a bike, or clipping a recipe from the newspaper—suddenly, the thought enters your mind that you are going to die."[4]

In fact, death is a more significant issue for middle-aged persons than it is for older people.[5] We spend more time thinking about it than do the ones who are closer to it.

As believers, we aren't supposed to be disturbed by the thought of dying, but many of us are. On the one hand we sing "When we all get to heaven" with gusto, and yet we devour self-help books that tell us how to have heaven on earth. We say we're ready to go, yet much of our anxiety about our health and medical benefits is due to our desire to cling to this present world. We talk about how wonderful heaven will be, but on days when we don't feel well and someone asks us how we are, we say, "Fine, considering the alternative."

If we're honest, we will admit to feeling ambivalent about death. I could lead Bible studies on the resurrected life, but when the hollow face of the Grim Reaper disturbed my dreams, I awakened in a cold sweat and felt the loneliness of the darkness. I didn't fear the actual process of dying, but I think that's what many are afraid of—the process, especially a painful one. I grieved the end of life as I know it here. Aware of dreams I wanted to pursue, I wanted to live!

We mature spiritually when we make peace with death. To come to this point of acceptance is not easy, but I believe it is an important goal. I know it is for me. I want to be a woman of fifty-eight, seventy-five, or eighty-three who is at peace with herself, who is growing and changing along with the world, and who's ready to pray, "Father, into Thy hands I commend my spirit" when it's time to die.

"The acceptance of death provides an irreplaceable wisdom about life and is a source of ultimate freedom."[6] It increases our appreciation for God's gift of life. It encourages us to make the most of the rest of our lives. It frees us to think about how we want to die.

As believers, we are on a pilgrimage; this world is not our final home. We are on a spiritual journey toward a heavenly destination. When we believe and accept this, we won't cling so desperately to this life and the things it offers. "The less attached we are to life, the more alive we can become."[7]

This was true of the women I surveyed. They talked of three benefits from their heightened awareness of the brevity of life and their mortality: an increased appreciation for life, a greater motivation to identify what was important to them, and a desire to use their time doing things that mattered to them.

Greater Appreciation for Life

Can you hear the gratitude in these words?

- "I enjoy life because I appreciate it more than ever. I observe more, and I listen more."
- "I want to enjoy the 'simple' life (less complicated, not so busy). I want to enjoy life's simple pleasures by taking time to smell the roses."
- "My husband died on the street. His heart stopped and two nurses came along and revived him. He had triple bypass surgery and is doing well, but there is so much disease in his heart that it's just a matter of time. It makes a person more thankful every day for the breath we have and to live every day as if it were the last day."
- "Having a chronic disease forced me to accept my own death and also gave me the need to make the time I have left on earth count in a meaningful way—a God-honoring way."
- "Scleroderma was a big wake-up call that screamed to me that I had a smaller amount of time than I thought and made me desire to spend the time left wisely."
- "As I have started losing those who are dear to me,

> I have felt freer to let others know how much they mean to me . . . while they are still alive."

As I grappled with my mortality, I too experienced a change. This was very evident in my morning prayers. My first words became: "Thank You, God, for another day. Thank You for life." One of the psalmists prayed, "So teach us to number our days, that we may apply our hearts unto wisdom" (Psalm 90:12, KJV). Counting our days is a way of noticing and valuing them—a way of showing gratitude that naturally leads to living wisely. "Father, help me to make the most of every minute." I recognized the preciousness of time; it was not to be wasted.

There's a bonus to lacing our days with gratitude: we worry less. As Janet wrote: "When I stop to observe, listen, and feel the present moment, I realize this is all I need to respond to today. Any anxiety I feel, whether it is about getting to a meeting on time or fear that I will wind up on the street in my old age, is quelled. This disposition allows me the freedom to go forward with what is in front of me, trusting that my relationships, spirituality, and even my financial security will evolve as an outgrowth of persevering in this awareness."

Pushes the Definition of Our Dream

Many people spend much of their lives indefinitely preparing to live. "Someday" we are going to write a book, change jobs, go to Europe, return to school, or remodel the kitchen. When the end of life is in sight, we feel that "someday" has arrived.

The woman who knows what she wants to do "someday" may have an advantage. She knows what she wants; the ticking of the clock may be just what she needs to get going on her dreams. Others of us, though, may want to do many things—too many things—and there's simply not enough time left to do it all. One woman wrote: "I want to retire or at least partly retire. My husband and I own and operate a pest control and insulation business and have for thirty-something years. The office is in our home. I keep books and handle sales. I feel like I'm always on duty. The last couple of years it has gotten really hard to keep everything going. I wish I had more time for myself, my hobbies, my grandchildren, and for ministry to others."

I identify with this woman. Up until midlife my dreams had always been nebulous. I finally realized that if any of them were going to come true, I had to define them. To do this, I asked myself, *What means the most to me? What do I want most to have accomplished or experienced before I die?*

What each of us wants varies. Women told me that over the next fifteen years they want to commit themselves to spiritual growth; to sustaining, deepening, improving, and strengthening relationships; to growing and learning; to professional development; and to gaining financial security. These are broad, general goals, and they need to be further defined. What *specifically* do we want? For example, what kind of financial security? A strong and padded savings account? Investments? The house paid for?

What do we see ourselves doing? What is important to us? Ten years from now, what kind of women do we want to be? In our discussion group, when we talked about this last question, one woman answered, "I want to be able to find my car at Wal-Mart." Keeping the mind working efficiently is important!

Another one said, "I want my husband to still find me sexy." We all chuckled, and as we did, we recognized the truth in what she said. For most of us the quality of our relationships—whether with our husband, children, grandchildren, or friends—will figure into the kind of person we want to be.

If you are going to know what matters most to you, you need to listen to your thoughts, sort them out, and weigh alternatives. You need to acknowledge your dreams and kindle your passions. You need to listen to God, discover what He wants, and receive His help—that's the only way to work in partnership with God and His power. And yet if you are like the women I surveyed, this is a major spiritual challenge. As one woman wrote: "Spending quality time with God is linked to my time management needs."

When time seems to be running out, how can you find time to define who you are, to dream, and to ask God how He wants to use you in the years ahead?

Finding Time

I've been helped by using these tried-and-true time management principles.

Prioritize. To identify which of my many interests are most important, I asked, *What do I want most to have accomplished or experienced by the time I die?* Reflecting on this question was so insightful that I wanted to include it in my survey, but some of my friends balked. They were not ready to look that far ahead!

Thinking in broad strokes helped me to prioritize, but May wanted something more focused on the present and more specific. She told me: "I embarked on a new organizer system so my scheduling is more controlled. With that, I set specific goals for the personal, spiritual, financial, family, and business areas I wish to pursue. Playing the piano on a regular basis was one of my specific personal goals. This was something I've been wanting to find time to do for years."

How you prioritize is not important. *Doing* it is. Prioritizing takes energy and focus, but it's essential for anyone who wants to make the most of the time she has.

Delegate. This is a time management term for engaging the help of others. While women are good at sensing the needs of others, we are often reluctant to ask for help. We need to ask ourselves, *Is there anything I'm presently doing that someone else in my family could do?* Engage their help, starting with these important words, "I need your help."

When Peggy, whom you met earlier, wanted to go back to school full-time, she and her husband were both concerned because of her scleroderma. Would she be able to keep up? She wanted to become a counselor. She needed to finish her bachelor's degree and get a master's degree. She didn't want to drag out her education by taking a course or two per semester. Could she handle a full college load and keep up with the housework? She and her husband thought not, so they hired their daughter (who was looking for a job) to take over home tasks.

Peggy said, "We hired our daughter to do all the housecleaning, laundry, some cooking, and to paint the trim on our house. It was wonderful to be able to focus all my time on school and not have the stress of taking care of the household chores."

Simplify. If you can't afford to hire help or are reluctant to persuade family members to help, simplifying your lifestyle may give you the extra time you need. Alice, who knows she needs to "take the time" because no one is going to give it to her, simplified her life in two ways. She wrote, "I sold my big old home where we had lived for twenty-plus years and moved into an upper flat with my sixteen-year-old daughter. No more yard work or snow removal—freedom! I've also decided I do not want to continue to try to climb the ladder in the workplace. I will stay at my same level of responsibility in order to have the freedom to pursue other interests."

Elizabeth, who has made several major positive changes since turning forty-five, says, "I have moved past wanting to acquire things. What-nots (dust collectors) are not nearly as important as I once thought they were. I am enjoying the freedom of living with less."

Many of us love to shop. Even as we trip over our latest acquisitions we head for the mall to buy more. "Things" demand attention: they must be dusted, stored, protected, and insured. Are they worth the long-term price? With fewer things, we can devote our time to adventure rather than maintenance.

We can also simplify our life by reducing our level of activity. The single most important time-management word is "no," as in, "No, I don't have time for that." "No" can be a hard word to say, but what do we gain in return? Precious time.

One woman said, "I consciously chose not to pursue the next rung on the career ladder to reduce the demands on my time and energy." Another wrote, "I simplified my lifestyle in order to be able to free myself from the burden of cumbersome possessions, which gives me the time to devote to spiritual growth and development, and exploring other paths."

Life Is a Gift

When we were young, we thought we had all the time in the world. Sometimes that mindset worked to our disadvantage. Many of us got sidetracked from fulfilling our dreams. A midlife awareness of the clock ticking can keep that from happening again if we will focus our energy on what is vital and important.

At the beginning of this chapter I mentioned one definition of middle age as the time when we start counting how many years we have left as well as how many years we have lived. My definition is, "You know you are middle-aged when you realize that life is a gift from God." We didn't do anything to deserve this gift, and we can't control how long we will have it. But we can control how we use the gift by managing our time wisely and linking our dreams with His.

CHAPTER ELEVEN

MEANING MATTERS

Why Am I Here?

I felt the power of the Lord was on me. He brought me out by the Spirit of the Lord. And he put me down in the middle of a valley. It was full of bones. The Lord led me around among the bones. There were many bones on the bottom of the valley. I saw the bones were very dry. Then he asked me, "Human being, can these bones live?"

Ezekiel 37:1-3, (ncv)

WHILE A GOOD FIRST STEP TOWARD BUILDING A DREAM FOR THE future lies in recognizing our potential, for many of us this isn't enough. We want something more; we want meaningful lives. In some way—large or small, public or private—we want to make a difference. We want a sense of purpose. We want lives that count. While this may be true of persons at any age, we become acutely aware of this need at midlife.

When we were in our twenties and early thirties—when life seemed to go on forever—it might not have occurred to us to contemplate the meaning of life. With the end in sight, meaning suddenly matters a great deal. Here are some of the things women said about this:

- "I want more understanding of the whole picture and how and where I fit in."
- "Does God truly desire a personal relationship with me? Does He actually have a purpose for each believer's life? Does what I do make a difference? Does He have meaningful work for me?"
- "I wonder what more I should be doing to make a difference."
- "I haven't felt I was clearly on the path I was born to walk; nearby, maybe, but not on it."
- "I want to be used by God. I do not only want to seek comfort and entertainment as many aging people do."

By the time we are in our forties and fifties, we have experienced losses that can leave us feeling lifeless and without purpose, as if our moorings have been cut.

LOSS HEIGHTENS OUR AWARENESS OF MEANING

Just as some respondents sang the joys of the empty nest, others regarded it as a time to find another meaningful purpose for the rest of their lives.

- "By forty-five I had successfully raised three wonderful children—all of a sudden I found myself floundering without goals and purpose for the rest of my life."
- "Having purpose in my life has become very important to me. In the child-raising years, I felt that my children and my family were my purpose for living. Now that my children are becoming independent, I feel a strong desire to pursue what else God has in store for me."
- "Since my only child got married, I have felt a need to become better focused on the purpose God has for my life."

Raising children is a purpose-driven activity and a consuming one. When actively parenting, you're conscious of your goal and the importance of what you are doing. You feel needed and productive. You're devoted to a goal. Even when it was frustrating, you still had the sense of living for something outside yourself. No wonder a woman might feel adrift when the intensity subsides.

Besides the loss of the parenting role, other midlife losses make us aware of our need for meaning: the loss of a mate, a job, or our health.

- "My inactivity due to chronic fatigue syndrome has caused me to feel a lack of purpose."
- "A floundering health causes me to continually reevaluate my resources available to God."
- "Much of the meaning of my life was peeled away when my husband divorced me."

Several losses may be involved. Doris's first career was in the military. She retired at age forty-four and took a job in civilian life. A year into her new job, she admitted to me how much she disliked it. She said, "I'm afraid to quit though. I don't want to shop around for another job. I mean, who is going to hire me at my age?"

When Doris left the military, she left behind that sense of being part of a bigger picture. She also lost her sense of structure. At the same time, she was losing her youth and she worried about being obsolete. She said, "I want—no, I *need*—a sense of purpose in my life." Doris needed to build a new dream.

MIDLIFE OBLIGATIONS

While loss can cause us to feel a lack of purpose, a sense of purposelessness may also result from having too much to do, particularly when doing for others. As one woman wrote, "I feel I'm floundering without a purpose because I don't feel in control. My time is tied up doing things for other people. It becomes mechanical just to get things done."

Cumulative problems can cause us to reflect upon what we're doing, why we're doing it, and if what we're doing has any value. Not long after Nan's husband lost his job, he suffered a heart attack. When he lost his job, he also lost their medical insurance. Medical bills stacked up. In a job that offered no chance of promotion, Nan felt the weight of their concerns. She plodded along, taking life a day at a time and reflecting as she went. "I look more closely at my position in life now and am a lot more critical. I look at where I fit into things. I look at what I am accomplishing in my job both personally and as a Christian. I look at my family and what I'm doing to benefit them as well as myself. I am critical of myself and often feel I don't do the right things or enough things, and then I wonder if I try to do too much! I am just not content with what I'm doing or accomplishing. I often feel I'm just existing, not living."

BEEN THERE, DONE THAT

Even the repetitiveness of what we do can create a sense of futility: going to work, doing the laundry, dusting, vacuuming, cooking, picking up, going to the same places, seeing the same people, and so on. Weariness settles in, as reflected in these comments.

- "Nothing surprises me anymore."
- "Is this as good as it gets?"
- "I've been there, done that, and I'm not interested."

Or, we find ourselves quoting the writer of Ecclesiastes, who also longed for a meaningful life. "What has been will be again, what has been done will be done again; there is nothing new under the sun" (1:9).

Strewn all over the valley of middlescence are bones—those items that seemingly keep us from feeling fully alive.

- Little time
- Empty nest
- Illness
- Divorce
- Changes
- Obligations
- Repetitiveness

As we look at the bones scattered about, we wonder, *Is there a meaningful life anywhere among them? Can these bones live?*

Valley of Validation

No doubt this same question was on the minds of God's people when they were in exile. They had been a people of purpose, chosen by God to be a light to the world and to live in the Promised Land. Now they were restless and discouraged, floundering in a foreign land. They said, "Our bones are dried up and our hope is gone; we are cut off" (Ezekiel 37:11, NCV).

But they weren't hopeless, and God wanted them to know that. He sent them Ezekiel. To affirm to Ezekiel that God's exiled people still had a significant future, God led Ezekiel to a valley filled with dry bones. God told him to prophesy to the bones, and then a miracle happened. Those brittle sticks of human structures arranged themselves into human skeletons. There they stood, a fleshless and lifeless army. But not for long. In fascination Ezekiel watched as they were rebuilt. Muscles appeared on the bones. Flesh grew, and skin covered the bones. At Ezekiel's command, the wind breathed on them, and the bones came to life.

What did this mean? It meant that the nation Israel would be resurrected and regenerated. The same possibility exists for us. Even though purpose seems to be escaping us, it is within our grasp. It is a matter of the mind, the heart, and the spirit.

SEEING THE POTENTIAL

Even though God's exiled people felt cut off—destroyed, they weren't. All the potential for being a people of purpose was still there; either they couldn't see it or refused to see it. If we want meaningful lives, we need to be mindful of our potential.

In her book, *Living a Purpose-Full Life*, Jan Johnson recommends data collecting as the first step in discovering your purpose.[1] This requires observing, gathering, and evaluating information about yourself. I hope this has been happening for you in this book. When we peeled back layered fears, what did you discover about yourself? When we listed the strengths of women over forty-five, did you identify your particular strengths?

When we look, listen, and gather, we find potential for what gives our lives meaning. We do not have to wait for better times or long for greener pastures. Right where we are, right now, purpose is possible.

If anybody could have been tempted to long for greener pastures, it was Saundra, whom you met in chapter 1. Saundra said, "Staying home and being a wife to a husband who didn't seem to like me or think of me as being valuable to him was not my definition of meaningful work. If I was going to continue in my marriage, I needed to be involved in work I found meaningful, fulfilling, and exciting."

Earlier—before this in-between time when she was trying to decide what she was going to do with the rest of her life—Saundra had had that kind of work. As she reflected on her past, she realized that God had equipped her for and given her a desire to work with people. Here are some things she noted in her journal about herself and her situation.

- "God used me when I raised my children."
- "God used me when I took a series of secretarial jobs to help out the family finances."
- "God used me when I worked with women in Bible studies over the years and I was privileged to lead several women to Christ."
- "I have a hunger to work with people, one on one, in a

way that could make a difference in their lives."
- "I have a difficult marriage, and yet an enduring one in which I have learned a great deal."

Over time—and this gathering process does take time—as Saundra mulled over her potential and prayed, it came to her that she could be a marriage and family therapist. Saundra hadn't even finished college, so to become a therapist would mean returning to school and facing several years of training. But the sense of being anchored returned when she envisioned who she could become and how she could have a meaningful life. Before the dream, she was constantly fighting depression and discouragement. After the dream, she felt alive and energized.

Recognizing who we are, what our situation is, and what we can do is an important component to living a meaningful life, but it is not the only component. Faith, hope, and obedience are also important.

Be a Messenger of Truth to Yourself

Through the "valley of dry bones" experience and other visions and words, Ezekiel was attempting to activate Israel's faith at God's initiative. When God said to Ezekiel, "Human, can these bones live?" (Ezekiel 37:3, NCV), Ezekiel responded, "Lord God, only you know." God put the ball back in Ezekiel's court. He said, "Prophesy to these bones" (verse 4).

In other words, "Be declarative, Ezekiel. Speak with the authority you have as a prophet. My people need confidence and hope. Inspire them with your actions and your words." The discouraged people needed their hope ignited and fueled if they were once again to be a people of purpose. Knowledge of potential is not enough.

How fortunate we are if we have an Ezekiel in our lives who creates within us a sense of possibility!

"You really know how to bring our church women together to work in unity. I'm glad God led you here, and I pray He will guide you as our leader."

"I've watched and observed you in our conference meetings.

You are a confident, decisive person. You quickly get right to the heart of any matter. Would you consider being our chairperson?"

"I've noticed what a good listener you are and how wise you are. Have you ever considered becoming a counselor?"

But a prophet isn't always around, so we may need to prophesy to ourselves, igniting and fueling our hope. The prophets were messengers of truth and hope, and we can speak that message to ourselves in various ways.

Talk to yourself. No, it's not crazy! Verbal feedback is a good spiritual tool for fighting negative feelings. In an Ezekiel tone, over and over say to yourself something like this: "God has a purpose for my life. I may not fully see it yet, but I know He is going to reveal it to me and enable me to do it."

Quote Scripture. Do this frequently and out loud. Quote a Bible verse about God's purpose for you. Put your name in it. Here's a sample: "'For I know the plans I have for you, (insert your name)' declares the LORD, 'plans to prosper you and not to harm you, plans to give you hope and a future'" (Jeremiah 29:11).

Pray expectantly. One of my frequent prayers comes from the prophet Jeremiah. "O great and powerful God, whose name is the LORD Almighty, great are your purposes and mighty are your deeds" (32:18-19). To which I add, "And I know You, God, are working out a purpose for my life."

Sing. The nation Israel proclaimed that they couldn't sing a song in a foreign land (see Psalm 137:4), but singing is a wonderful hope activator. I can't think of anything better for us to sing while we're in the middlescent valley than the words to an old spiritual, "Dem bones, dem bones, dem . . . dry bones!" Close the drapes, dance to the music, and sing with gusto, because the truth is that middlescent bones can and will rise again!

HOW MUCH DO YOU WANT TO HEAR GOD?

When God's people complained of their bones drying up, they were describing a spiritual condition. Their souls were dry. To remedy this, God instructed Ezekiel to say to the bones (which symbolized the people), "Dry bones, hear the word of the LORD (Ezekiel 37:4)." On many occasions, the nation Israel heard what the prophets were saying, as in "Testing 1, 2, 3. Can you hear me?" but still they didn't *hear* God.

"Hearing the word of the Lord" involves a consciousness of God. We must be aware of Him—who He is and His realness. We seek His voice through prayer, Bible study, meditation, solitude, worship, and providential circumstances. A sensitivity develops that keeps us ever listening for His words. When He speaks, we respond in obedience (see John 14:23).

Fortunately, Saundra's bones weren't dry. Like a sunflower following the sun, she turned naturally to God throughout her life, something I always admired about her. When she began thinking about what she wanted to do with the rest of her life, she turned to God. "I told God I desired to be used by Him. I told Him I needed a goal to focus on, not just my disappointing relationship with my husband. However, if He wanted me to pour out my entire life for Harry, I would. I knew I could do it with God's daily help. I asked God to close doors if it was not His will for me to go back to school to pursue a career in counseling."

The spiritual part of finding my purpose didn't come as naturally to me as it did for Saundra. While I was aware of my potential and could sing "Dem Dry Bones" with fervor, I had one spiritual ear closed—something I was unaware of, which I will share more about in chapter 13.

Others of us don't want to expend the effort involved in hearing God's voice because it's work. One woman said, "I have felt that I'm floundering without clear purpose and often use my business to fill the gap rather than coming to grips with this and trying to remedy it."

Doris would be the first to admit that she identifies with the dry bones metaphor. She can still remember the spiritual hunger she felt in her college and young adult days—how God-conscious she was. Sometimes when she is driving to work, she thinks about it. Where did her fervency go? She longs for purposeful living, but when she gets home in the evening, she reads, watches television, and sometimes plays computer games. She admitted, "I tell myself I deserve a few hours of time to do nothing after my years of regimented living, but I'm distracting myself from listening to God."

What Doris and I—and others who are searching for meaning—

have to ask ourselves is, *How much do I want it? Do I want it enough to honor God and be obedient?*

Meaning is found in reverencing and obeying God; it fulfills the purpose for which we were created (see Ecclesiastes 12:13). We feel in sync with Him and feel that we are a part of something much larger than we can see and fully comprehend. The nation Israel would never be able to fulfill their purpose unless they were obedient, and neither can we.

THE BREATH OF VITALITY

When Ezekiel prophesied to the bones as God had commanded, he suddenly heard a loud noise followed by the clicking of the bones. There was a noise and a rattling. The bones came together, muscles came on the bones, flesh grew, and skin covered the bones. "But there was no breath in them" (Ezekiel 37:8, NCV). Although the bodies had been restored, they were still not alive because they had no breath.

Then God said to Ezekiel, "Prophesy to the [breath]. . . 'This is what the LORD GOD says: [O breath,] come from the four winds, and breathe on these people who were killed so they can come back to life'" (verse 9). At creation, God formed the man from clay and breathed into his nostrils the breath of life (see Genesis 2:7). Then the man lived. The account is similar here. Ezekiel prophesied as God commanded, and breath entered them; they came to life and stood on their feet (verse 10).

When mind, heart, and spirit line up together in our lives, a time will come when we'll hear the clicking of those dry bones strewn around in the middlescent valley. An excitement will bubble up within us. *Ah, yes, they're coming together!* Then God will breathe vitality into us, and we'll discover there is indeed life after forty—life filled with meaning and purpose.

CHAPTER TWELVE

FAITH FOR THE FUTURE

Is It Possible to Have a Vibrant but Not Naïve Faith?

I believe that seeking God's will and following it requires surrender and trust—a constant challenge—so I immerse myself in His Word and promises. Do I believe them? Do they work? Why not find out?

JUDY PETERSON, AUTHOR AND SURVEY RESPONDENT

CARILEEN'S CHILDREN DIDN'T TURN OUT AS SHE EXPECTED AND dreamed; two of them chose values completely contrary to hers. She now questions the validity of Bible promises such as "Train a child in the way he should go, and when he is old he will not turn from it" (Proverbs 22:6). She wonders, *If I couldn't count on God's promises to be fulfilled in young adulthood, how can I claim His promises for the future?*

When adolescents are thinking about what they're going to do with the rest of their lives, they don't have a backlog of old issues that dampen their confidence in God. By the time we are in midlife, however, our experiences over the past forty years directly affect the quality of our faith. For some, life's story line took a different turn than expected. Their faith was challenged by the death of a spouse or child, an unwanted and unexpected divorce, sudden job loss, and so on.

- "My dear husband (and best friend) died very suddenly. He and I had been together since we were fifteen years old; we were married for thirty-two years. This pretty much destroyed my happiness and severely shook my faith. I guess I'm a bit afraid to trust God again. . . . I was always very sure of the promise of heaven/life everlasting/eternal happiness. Now I worry about that promise and pray for reassurance. . . . My faith has been sorely shaken."
- "I watched my Mom and Dad suffer before their deaths. My husband's mother died of cancer, and I took care of his mentally ill aunt for fifteen years. I ached with my son and granddaughters through a divorce. These are the difficult years; my young adult years were the happy ones."
- "The last several years there have been so many deaths of family and friends that I find myself anxious when the phone rings. I'm trying to give it to God, but I'm not always successful."

- "My understanding of the church's teaching about marriage and the home, plus those on the role of women in the church and in society set me up to be a victim in all those areas. Since my divorce, I have taken a good hard look at them and concluded that many of those teachings were sincere but misguided. That has opened a Pandora's box of questions about many other things I was taught to believe."

These women experienced a devastating loss of some kind—a loss that affected their ability to trust God. Other women speak about heartaches as parents.

If I Do Everything Right, My Kids Will Turn Out Right

We were such earnest parents. We studied what the Bible said about families and we prayed. We devoured magazines and self-help books. We went to conferences and raised our children by the best advice. We took them to church and made sure they were involved in activities. We convinced ourselves of this thought: *If I do everything right, my children will turn out right.* But some of us have discovered that despite our best efforts, our children can disappoint us.

- "My twenty-six-year-old daughter's life is a mess (spiritually, financially, and in her relationships)."
- "I believe my greatest spiritual challenge has been in maintaining my faith and spiritual focus in parenting teenagers and young adults."
- "My kids accepted Christ as children, but now two of them do not serve Him wholeheartedly, and one not at all. They are disillusioned with the organized church."
- "Since turning forty-five, I've been busy helping to develop a sense of spirituality in my children. Some days I'm frustrated as I've watched two of them leave the denomination of their childhood."

- "I am impatient with my children when they don't see the importance of putting God first."
- "My daughter-in-law's father said to me, 'I think it's wonderful to get to this stage of having our children raised and feel good about it.' I didn't answer him because I didn't feel good about it. My daughters want to be free, but they don't realize what it costs my husband and me to set them free."

One woman wrote: "Where did it all go wrong? My son slammed himself into a searing fire that I would have cut off my hands to save him from." A mischievous prank got him into serious trouble with the law in a way that his future will always be affected, and yet this mother tried so hard to prepare him for a bright future. Her words remind me of King David's words when he heard the news of Absalom's death: "O my son Absalom! My son, my son Absalom! If only I had died instead of you—O Absalom, my son, my son!" (2 Samuel 18:33).

Even when the circumstances aren't as tragic as King David's, disappointed parents instinctively identify with his grief; and even though these parents may not be in any danger of abandoning their faith, the quality of their faith has suffered.

Disappointment in the Church

I was surprised by the number of women in the survey who expressed disappointment in the family of God—in their fellow Christians and members of the clergy. I was looking for answers that included a search for meaning, authenticity, and freedom—issues that paralleled what I was reading; I hadn't thought about disappointment in believers as a midlife concern. This was not an issue expressed by a majority of women, but it was listed enough times that I felt it needed to be included here because disappointment with other Christians can affect our relationship with God.

- "After I asked for help in a group of fifteen people (I had started the group in my church), not one person called. I decided to live my life away from Christians but not from God. I am trying to get back to Bible study, but I don't want to get very involved because of my deep hurt."

- "I've gone through a period of depression because of being hurt by Christians in different areas of my life—things I would have expected from the world but not from brothers and sisters in Christ."
- "My biggest spiritual challenge has been disappointment in churches, ministers, and in seeing people on fire for the Lord who then turn their backs on God."
- "I struggle with cynicism resulting from disappointment in the actions of people I believed to be strong in the faith."
- "I have a very real struggle with my attitude toward my pastor, with whom I'm very dissatisfied, and I know this affects my spiritual growth."
- "After attending the same church for over fifteen years (and not only being very active in many areas, but also later working as the church secretary), I left the church to preserve what was left of my faith. The leaders of the church caused me great spiritual unrest and pain."
- "I have been taught from childhood to look to clergy for spiritual nourishment. Now I find myself often alone in search of answers, not being satisfied with the clergy available to me."

Some women responded to their disappointments by withdrawing from the Christian community; they left to avoid further hurt. Those who remained wonder, *How can I have a childlike trust in God when I am no longer naïve?*

My Faith Just Isn't What It Used to Be

When we get bogged down by life's unexpected turns, parental heartaches, disappointments, and the cares of life, our faith may suffer from defeatism. It loses its vitality, just as muscle loses its strength when it isn't exercised. "Faith not only enables growth, it also is subject to its own growth and maturity."[1] If we want to dream of a future filled with meaning and where we can fully use our potential, then we need a growing faith.

Pastor James Bolejack discovered the need for a growing faith when he studied middle-agers in the church for his doctoral dissertation. "The project participants often expressed faith in terms of a stabilizing, sustaining power in their life. However, the members apparently had little experience with faith as a power to become. This quality of faith is essential to true faith and the continuation of a meaningful pilgrimage."[2]

A staying faith is one that comforts. It sustains us through life's unexpected turns and disappointments. We all want and need this kind of faith, but if we are to make the most of our potential and have a purposeful life, we need more. We need *faith to become* the women God is calling us to be. We need a growing faith.

Faith Development

Imagine your faith as a plant in need of attention and yourself as the clay pot that holds the plant. No offense intended! Paul refers to believers as "common clay pots" (2 Corinthians 4:7, TEV).

For some time now you've noticed the plant isn't thriving. It droops; the leaves are turning yellow and dropping off, and it isn't growing. You could just throw the plant out, but suppose a dear friend gave it to you. You want to keep it because you treasure the friendship, so you know what you have to do: clean out the clay pot, repot the plant, and nurture it. To clean out the pot you gently work the plant out of the soil and lay it aside. Then you dig out the old dirt, scrape the mineral deposits off the pot, and wash it with soap and water.

Reviving our faith begins with a similar process. We clean out our souls. We dig out old faith-related hurts, scrape off hardened faith-interfering deposits, and wash the inner person clean. We dig out the old hurts with the intention that we are going to let them go. The soil of our hurts discouraged our faith rather than nurtured its growth. It's time to ask, *Am I willing to let go of my disappointment with God? Am I willing to really trust Him again?*

Strong emotions such as anger, grief, sadness, and resentment are usually associated with our disappointment in God and fellow believers. Like mineral deposits, they attach themselves to the soul, crowding out valuable growing space. We can scrape off these emotion deposits by expressing them in healthy ways, such as the ways described in chapters 3 and 6. One woman told me she used "honest praying" when she found out her grandson had cerebral palsy. She admitted how she felt and poured out her feelings to God. She wrote, "The sorrow was so great. I cried out to God. I can honestly say that God answered. My grandson is nine years old now and such a joy to me."

While we are scraping off hardened emotional deposits, we need to look for other items to clean out. We may need to deal with sin, unforgiveness, or our desire to know why.

The sin deposit. We first alluded to sin in chapter 6 when we looked at our erratic emotions and suggested that sin might be a possible explanation. While guilt wasn't mentioned, it is a strong emotion and one we experience following disobedience. Guilt prompts us to blame others instead of taking responsibility. Adam and Eve both blamed others when they disobeyed God in the Garden. Eve blamed the serpent (see Genesis 3:1-13). Adam, though, didn't blame only Eve, he made God responsible. When God confronted him, Adam said, "The woman *you* put here with me—she gave me some fruit from the tree, and I ate it" (Genesis 3:12, emphasis added).

If we are going to clean out our souls and be really honest with ourselves, some of us may need to ask, *Am I blaming God and calling it disappointment in Him, when I bear some responsibility?* I had to deal with this question. In my heart I held God responsible for my lack of success, and it cast a shadow over my faith.

The unforgiveness deposit. A sin we may cherish is unforgiveness; we can't forgive those people who have wronged us or disappointed us. Our unforgiveness may be justified, but what is it doing to our faith? Will it keep it from growing? Will it keep us from experiencing a meaningful life? It doesn't matter whether someone deserves forgiveness; we deserve to have a clean space for our faith to thrive.

When we've had experiences that jolt our faith, we may need

to forgive God. He doesn't need our forgiveness in the sense that He did something wrong (once we see the full picture we may be able to understand what happened to us), but we may need to forgive God in order to trust our future to Him.

The "Why?" deposit. Job was a man who suffered, and he was certain that sin was not to blame. He said, "I am *not* a sinner—I repeat it again and again" (Job 27:6, TLB). Job wanted to know why he suffered, and he longed for an audience with God (see Job 23:1–24:25). If we just knew why, we are certain we could handle life's unexpected turns and be at peace.

When God stepped into the dialogue between Job and his friends (see Job 38:1–41:34), He spoke in such a way that Job recognized that God's purposes are often beyond human understanding but they are not evil (42:2-3). God vindicated Job by rebuking the friends who had been so critical of Job, and He replaced what Job had lost (verses 7-9,10-14); *but* He didn't tell Job why he suffered. If we want our faith to be renewed, we may have to relinquish our need to know. This doesn't mean we will never find out; it just means that we will quit allowing what happened to impede the development of our faith.

God blessed the latter part of Job's life more than the first (Job 42:12). We want God's blessing on the second half of our lives too. This may mean that we'll have to choose to move on without knowing why we had to experience what we did.

REPLANTING FAITH

Once we've cleaned out the soul, it's time to replant our faith. We do this by recommitting ourselves to Jesus Christ. Jesus said, "I am the resurrection and the life" (John 11:25). He can bring new life to our faith when we turn to Him with the same simple commitment with which we began our Christian walk.

Oleta told me, "I was totally changed at the age of forty-three. Up until that time, I was not allowing God to have control of my life. I made the decision to surrender my life to God and to make Jesus the Lord of my life. He is now my Savior and my Lord. He gave me a new nature and new desires. It is so exciting to serve Him. My ministry is music, and I enjoy singing in our church and other churches. I enjoy going on crusades to other countries and encouraging Christians who are less fortunate financially. God has given me a love and a passion for this. I have been to the Ukraine twice, and it has given me a global view of the world and the urgency to share the gospel. I am now fifty-six years old, and the happiest years of my life have been the last thirteen."

When we recommit ourselves to Jesus, when we accept what He says about God and about life, and when we stake everything on Him, our faith will be revitalized.

NURTURING OUR FAITH

If we want our faith to thrive, we need to nurture it. Here are some ways to do that:

Choosing a disciplined Bible study (see 1 Peter 2:2). If you study the Bible with others, choose a study where effort matters. Tossing clichés around at each session will not nurture faith. God wants to speak to us through His Word, and He will when we involve ourselves. You may discover that the way the Bible was interpreted to you in the past was damaging to your faith. In a disciplined Bible study, we may discover what the Bible really says.

Associating with believers who have a "becoming" faith. Listen to the prayer requests of others in the groups you are a part of. Do their requests reflect a *becoming* faith or a *staying* faith? There's nothing wrong with praying for comfort, but if that is all people are concerned with, you may feel the same. Join groups that have members who are ready to tackle challenges and to pray with boldness (see Acts 4:23-31).

Exercising your faith. Volunteer to do something that makes you uneasy or stretches you so that you have to rely on God. Go on a missions trip, participate in an outreach effort, or try a new way of worshiping. Many of our efforts go toward making our lives comfortable and secure; but sometimes a little insecurity is just what we need to build a strong faith muscle.

Dr. Carol Pierskalla, program director of American Baptist National Ministries' Aging Today and Tomorrow program, says, "At some point we must deal with the fact that bad things happen to us, even though God loves and cares for us. As we experience life's blows, our faith must stretch to provide a context for loss and disappointment. If a person's faith is the same as it was when she or he was twenty-five, it's not going to be adequate for that person as an older adult. Faith must be dynamic and must change to accommodate what happens to us as we get older."[3]

When we clean out the clay pot of our soul and replant our faith and nurture it, we will develop a *dynamic, growing* faith. We'll have a faith that will enable us to dream of what we can be and to pursue that vision, trust in God, and experience a meaningful life.

CHAPTER THIRTEEN

FREE AT LAST, FREE AT LAST

How Do I Reconcile My Will with God's Will?

Honor God and obey his commands. This is the most important thing people can do.

Ecclesiastes 12:13 (NCV)

As I worked through the questions in this book, a new self emerged. A more confident self. A woman aware of who she was and what her strengths were. A more assertive woman. I liked her.

I liked her so much that I resisted the idea of surrendering this new self to God, something I was reminded of when I happened to read *Victory Through Surrender* by E. Stanley Jones. He notes: "The Christian faith in its New-Testament form asks nothing less and nothing more than self-surrender to God."[1] I knew this was true because Jesus said, "If anyone wishes to be a follower of mine, he must leave self behind" (Luke 9:23, NEB), but I balked. *How can I surrender my self to God when I just discovered I have a self?*

If anyone had talked to me about self-awareness when I was younger, I would not have had a clue what she was talking about. My life was all wrapped up in the lives of others because this was how I thought God wanted me to live. I wanted to please Him even more than I wanted to please others. But now I wondered, *Will God want me to keep putting others first? Will I have to keep my dreams on the back burner?*

I faulted God for my lack of success—I'd had few speaking engagements, infrequent publications, and was unable to support myself. It wasn't that I hadn't tried, but most of the doors I knocked on stayed closed. I assumed that God had closed them. *What about the future? Will God continue to close doors?*

As I was struggling with surrendering my newfound self, my friend Katie was going through something similar and even more challenging.

Wrestling with Obedience

Katie had suffered from extremely low self-esteem throughout her life. Her usual mental response to compliments was, *If you knew who I really was, you would not think well of me.* She was afraid that if she looked people in the eye they would see the real Katie, the awful Katie.

She also happened to be in a disappointing marriage. Just seven months into the marriage, her husband stopped making love to her. When Katie asked him why, he simply said, "You don't excite me anymore." She had gained a few pounds, so she lost weight. When that didn't produce results, her pain was intense. She blamed herself. *If I were a lovable and worthwhile woman, my husband wouldn't treat me this way.*

From time to time throughout her marriage, she begged Al to go to counseling with her. Sometimes he would go with her for a session or two but never stay with it. They even took a marriage enrichment course together, and Al joked his way through the classes. The other participants loved him, while Katie could barely sit through the classes without crying.

Katie said, "To the world, my husband and I kept up the image that we were the perfect couple. In public, he held my hand and put his arm around me. His treatment of me in private, though never physically abusive, reinforced my feelings of worthlessness. Still, he provided a home and security for me, and I clung to our marriage, feeling like I didn't even deserve that."

When her mother died, Katie went to a therapist to get help through her grief. Soon the counseling sessions moved past her grief to her low self-esteem. Katie revealed that she had been sexually molested as a child and again as a teenager. As she worked through these experiences with the counselor's help, she realized that she had always felt responsible for the abuse . . . that she had brought it upon herself. All of her life she had blamed herself, thinking she was a terrible person and didn't deserve anyone's love. Now at age forty-five, God opened her eyes to the truth about herself. She saw herself as He sees her. She wasn't to blame for the abuse; the sin lay at the feet of her abusers.

Discovering this truth changed Katie, raising her self-esteem and helping her to appreciate who she is. She began to accept compliments and take joy in her accomplishments. When people talked to her, she looked them in the eye. But Katie told me that the healing of her heart brought with it a new challenge: "Now I was frustrated with my marriage. I was furious with Al for refusing to get help and for making me feel the problems in our marriage were my fault. Once I realized I had a right to expect more from our marriage, I was frustrated and unhappy.

"I asked Al one more time to go see a counselor with me. This time he just said, 'No.' I was so angry I wanted to run away, and I fantasized about it for weeks. Yet I believed with all my heart that what God had joined together no one should put asunder (see Mark 10:9). When I married, I vowed before God that I would be committed to Al as long as we both were alive (see Matthew 5:33-37; James 5:12). I wanted to leave, but what did God want?"

Katie's circumstances were more difficult than most; I tell her story to demonstrate that obedience is an ongoing struggle in the Christian life. I used to think that the older I got the more spiritual I would become and that obedience would come naturally. Not true. Obedience continues to be a challenge for us at midlife because our circumstances are changing, and we are changing. Like me, you probably know people who are tired of the struggle and have given up: a single friend grows tired of remaining celibate and moves in with her boyfriend. A married relative who has endured a boring marriage for years opts for excitement. In her forties, she meets someone on the Internet and has an affair.

Many people give up because obedience is hard. As one respondent said, "I long ago surrendered my will to God's will, but sometimes I take the white flag back and shred it."

How, then, can we stay engaged in the struggle? How can we reconcile our will with God's will?

RECONCILING THE TWO

I don't believe there is a works-every-time, step-by-step formula for aligning our wills with God's will. Many variables are involved. Our circumstances and our personalities vary. Some people find obedience easier than others do. Nevertheless, we all struggle with obedience at times, so here are some suggestions for bringing your will into alignment with God's.

Study the Bible. When we're fighting it, God's will can seem loathsome and limiting. Earnest Bible study can change our perspective.

We can see that doing God's will is connected with purpose. When God called the Israelites, He said, "Now if you obey me fully and keep my covenant, then out of all nations you will be my treasured possession . . . you will be for me a kingdom of priests and a holy nation" (Exodus 19:5-6). Once they were in the land God gave them, they were continually tempted to be disobedient, as the book of Judges tells us; they were particularly vulnerable to idolatry. Along the way, numerous prophets reminded them: "You either shape up and live the way God wants you to live or you will lose your land."[2] By the time Ezekiel spoke to them about his vision of the dry bones (see Ezekiel 37), they had lost the land. Even if their faith was revived and their hope ignited by Ezekiel, being a people of purpose was still going to be dependent on obedience (see Ezekiel 18:19; 33:14-16). They never could quite become what God called them to be because they were disobedient.

God speaks to us through His Word and woos us to follow Him. The Bible reassures us of God's love for us. To the Israelites, God's commandments may have seemed too harsh. The Israelites may have believed He expected too much. Sometimes when we are resisting God's will, we may think the same thing. We may even think He deliberately wants to make life difficult, but the Bible makes it clear that God's motive is love. As Moses prepared the Israelites for claiming the land God had promised them, he reminded them over and over of God's love for them (see Deuteronomy 4:37; 7:7-8; 13; 10:15; 23:5; 33:3). The good news is that God loves those who are obedient and He loves those who are sinners (see Psalm 146:8; Proverbs 15:9; 2 Corinthians 9:7; Romans 5:8; Ephesians 2:4-5; and Titus 3:4-5).

We may discover we have been wrong in our interpretation of God's will. If I had read the Bible more closely, I might have seen that I didn't always have to put others first. Jesus' life was wrapped up with people and their needs, but there were also times when He put His needs first. When His popularity exploded at Capernaum, which would have given Him an opportunity to minister to increasing numbers of people, Jesus got up early in the morning and went off to a solitary place to pray (see Mark 1:35). When Jesus heard the news about the death of John the Baptist, He left the crowd and went by boat to a lonely place (see Matthew 14:13). Luke said Jesus often withdrew to lonely places (Luke 5:16).

I must have closed my spiritual eyes along with my spiritual ear!

Persist in honest prayer. Reova, a woman who started a center for women's ministries at age fifty-two, was directed by God to deal with her anger with her husband. Reova had been in a less than quality marriage, for which her husband blamed her. Her frustration with her marriage and the lack of help for Christian women such as herself was part of her motivation for starting the center. But as she studied Colossians 3:5-14, God asked her to remove the anger and malice she felt toward her husband. The passage is about putting to death every part of ourselves that is against God and keeps us from fulfilling the will of God; it admonishes believers to get rid of anger, wrath, malice, blasphemy, and filthy communication. God said to Reova, "If you want, you can be angry with your husband the rest of your life. There's a part of your ministry, though, that I will never be able to develop until you get rid of it."

The Colossians passage also gives a list of graces that we are to wear as "clothing." As Reova studied "Bear with each other and forgive whatever grievances you may have against one another. Forgive as the Lord forgave you. And over all these virtues put on love, which binds them all together in perfect unity" (Colossians 3:13-14), God revealed to her how to pray. Each morning as she put on her makeup, she prayed, "Father, take away the anger, forgive my grievance, help me to love Doug and bring unity into this marriage." And she added—here's where the honesty comes in—"I don't want You to do this." Her anger shielded her from being vulnerable again. She didn't want to give up that protective shield. So she was honest about her reluctance, *but* she continued to pray. After three weeks of praying this way, her heart began to change and she dropped the words, "I don't want You to do it." Six months later, the anger was gone.

Vent the accompanying emotions. Surrendering to God's will is a spiritual struggle; but often our emotions get in the way. When we vent these emotions, our resistance often diminishes. Marian, a friend from graduate school days, knows the value of expressing her emotions when struggling with God's will. She said, "Crying and just allowing myself to be before God in my hurt and frustration and yes, anger, allows Him to wrap me in His arms and give me security and the ability to abide in His will."

Talking about your feelings can also help you work through your resistance. Be sure you choose someone safe—a wise friend, your pastor, or a counselor. Katie talked with her counselor. She said, "Within the confines of his office, I was able to express my frustration, anger, and unhappiness over my marriage. At first I just let myself experience the disappointment and sadness I felt. That was critical to my eventually being able to release those negative feelings. Gradually I realized I had a choice to make: Would I remain in the marriage or not?"

In addition to providing a safe place for venting our feelings, talking may give us additional insight about God or about ourselves. This insight alone may be enough to bring us to surrender.

Weigh the alternatives. Ask yourself: *What happens if I don't submit? What happens if I do?* We can live comfortable lives—even exciting lives—without being obedient, but can we grow spiritually? Can we experience the refreshing and supportive presence of the Holy Spirit? Do we want to be at peace with God?

The apostle Paul said, "Let the peace of God be the decider of all things within your heart" (Colossians 3:15, Barclay).[3] When feelings clash, when wills compete, when we are torn in two directions, we experience inner turmoil—inner wrestling, agitation, disharmony. When we align our wills with God's will, the agitation and turmoil cease. The harmony in our relationship returns, and we are at peace with God.

In my case, I stewed for weeks, weighing the alternatives, until I admitted that I wanted the peace of God more than I wanted my will. Marian observed, "Being in His will gives me a 'resting place.'" Indeed, it does, and I wanted that more than anything.

Eventually decide. A time comes when you have to make a decision: Will I obey God? You may have studied your Bible, cried, prayed, talked, and stewed, and still not have surrendered your will. Obedience is an act of the will—your will.

Katie made her decision just prior to her twenty-fifth wedding anniversary. She said, "My counselor helped me see my alternatives. He had me look at the consequences of staying married and at the consequences if I chose to leave. He made it clear that neither choice would be ideal, but that it was a choice I would have to make. It was not an easy decision. In the end, I decided to stay in the marriage because I knew it was God's will for me. God convinced me that He would meet all of my needs 'according to His riches in glory.' It was a long and difficult process, but because I allowed myself to honestly wrestle with God, I was able to choose to stay married. Knowing that I'm not stuck, but that I'm in this marriage because I choose to be, makes all the difference in the world. While our marriage is definitely not all I would like it to be, I am content and at peace."

AFTER SURRENDER

Jesus said, "Unless a grain of wheat falls into the ground and dies, it remains a single grain. But if it dies, it yields a great harvest" (John 12:24, WMS). We hold the seed of self-will in our hands. When we resist God's will, we clench our fists around it and hold it tightly in our grasp. But when we bury the seed—die to self and submit our will to God's will—new growth will emerge. A new life will grow and produce many seeds in the way of unforeseen blessings.

For example, in choosing to stay married, Katie has more ministry opportunities than she would otherwise have—something she values and finds fulfilling. Content in her marriage, she now understands her husband better. She said, "I see now that Al is struggling with self-esteem issues similar to mine, though I don't know the reasons. My counselor helped me to see that Al doesn't reject me because I'm a terrible person. Rather, it is because he feels so badly about himself that he will not allow himself to be intimate with me. And because I now know I am a person of worth, I can appreciate my husband's good qualities. I understand that he will have to struggle with issues in his life just as I have had to, but his struggles are not a reflection on me."

On this side of surrender, Katie is a happier person: "Besides a new relationship with my husband, I am now able to open myself to new and deeper relationships with friends, and I have found new ways to enjoy life. In surrendering to God, my self-esteem was strengthened. Because I willingly submitted to Him, I no longer see myself as a victim. I no longer see myself as a dirty person or a total failure. My new self is doing more, loving more, and enjoying more than I have in my entire life. Free from anger and resentment, I am free to fully enjoy relationships. I am free to be me; I don't have to hide my real self anymore."

Reova found that once she was free of the anger and malice she had held in her heart, God kept His promise to develop her ministry. Today there are six more centers ministering to women in the United States, and she is currently thinking of going global.

When I submitted my will to God, I prayed, "Okay, God, I give You my newly discovered self. I am Yours to do with as You please." In the days afterward, my daily prayer became, "God, what do You want me to do?" God answered, as He did to Elijah, in a still small voice (see 1 Kings 19:12). "You are on the right track. I want you to be My spokeswoman. Continue to write and to speak."

This coming together of my will and God's will—making them one and the same—has helped me immensely. When I come to a discouraging hurdle in the pursuit of my dreams, I attempt to jump over it because I'm convinced I'm doing God's will. When I step up on a platform to speak and wonder if anyone will listen to me, I remind myself that I'm there because God wants me there. When I meet a new editor for the first time and wonder if my age will be a detriment, I remind myself that God wants me to write. When I worry about all the youthful competition, I remind myself that God has given me something to say.

But this confidence is not the best part; there's more. The shadow that hung over my faith dissipated. To be a spokeswoman for God, and to learn and do it well, I joined the National Speakers Association. Through my membership, I learned that God hadn't closed as many doors as I had thought. NSA gave me a broader view of what is involved in speaking and in getting opportunities. I had been naïve. Once I learned how the system works, I could look back at opportunities I had missed simply because I hadn't taken initiative or because I hadn't known what to do. At other times, I had failed to knock harder when doors of opportunity were cracked open. God, I discovered, was not at fault for my lack of success.

I felt so free. I was reminded of Jesus' words, "If you hold to my teaching, you are really my disciples. Then you will know the truth, and the truth will set you free" (John 8:31-32). I joined freedom's chorus ("Free at last, free at last") when I discovered myself, but I sang louder and more fervently when God helped me to see the truth about myself and how I might better partner with Him to accomplish His purpose in my life.

I don't know if I would have learned this had I not been obedient. Rather than restricting me as I feared, obedience has allowed me to be more fully myself. "It is a paradox, but you are never so much your own than when you are most His. . . . You suddenly realize that you have aligned yourself with the creative forces of the universe so you are free—free to create, free to love, free to live at your maximum, free to be, to be all He wills you to be."[4]

CHAPTER FOURTEEN

I HAVE A DREAM

How Can I Build a Vision for My Future?

Now faith is the turning of dreams into deeds. . . .

Hebrews 12:1 (Cotton Patch Version)[1]

WHEN PAM'S PASTOR ASKED HER TO ATTEND A CHURCH LEADER-ship conference, she reluctantly agreed to go; she felt emotionally drained from her son's recent wedding. The preparations had been tedious because her son married into a family she wasn't comfortable with, plus she hated giving him up. Her only other child, another son, had been killed in an accident when he was fifteen years old. She grieved over her second son's leaving home.

A speaker who held retreats for women hosted one of the conference workshops. As Pam listened to her talk about issues important to women, an urge to do the same swelled within her. She thought, *I can do what she does. I can lead retreats. I can help women.*

Pam went back to her home church, organized women's retreats, and began discipling younger women. Four years and four retreats later, I met Pam. I was drawn to her because she bubbled with enthusiasm and vibrancy.

Ah, that building a vision for our future would be that simple for all of us! Pam was ripe, and the vision came quickly and clearly. Most of us develop a vision over time as we sort through what's important to us, what we want to accomplish, and what God wants. A vision develops as a by-product of this mental and spiritual work. As you've been answering the questions in the last five chapters, I hope a vision has been forming in your mind of who you can be and what you can do. Now we need to think about making that mental image come to life. How can we transfer that picture from the dream world to the real world?

TRANSFERRING THE DREAM

My mother embroidered pillowcases when I was a child. The process fascinated me. She would get her iron really hot, unfold the carbon-lined pattern of what she wanted to embroider, lay it on the pillowcase, and press that hot iron on it. Instantly the picture appeared, and then she began working with her threads of greens, blues, reds, and yellows to create a beautiful picture.

Before we build our dream, we need to transfer the vision from our head to somewhere we can see it, then embroider it and bring it to life. I recommend starting with putting your vision on paper. Take what you have in your head and write it down. If you have trouble getting started, here are some ways to begin.

- "In my fifties and sixties, I want to be . . . or I want to do . . . "
- "By the time I'm seventy-five, I want to . . . "
- "In my mind I see myself as a woman who is . . . and who will . . . "
- "Over the next twenty years, I want to commit myself to . . . "

Don't worry about punctuation or grammar; no one is going to see this but you. Don't worry about it if you have trouble getting all your vision down. Write what comes naturally. Let it sit, and then go back over it from time to time to revise and add to it until you are satisfied you have your dream on paper.

If at first you can't express it in sentences, just write descriptive phrases or words—something like these.

- Financial security
- Mentoring young women
- More time for music
- Growing and learning
- Sustaining relationships
- Changing careers
- Going back to school

If you prefer, cut out pictures from magazines and newspapers of women you admire or of women in a situation you would like to be in. Put them in a notebook, paste them on poster board, or pin them on your bulletin board. Glance at these pictures often. Hold them in your hand and look at them as you pray.

Whether you start with sentences, phrases, or pictures, the important thing is that your internal vision becomes an external vision. As you study your vision on paper, you may want to make changes to it or rewrite it, or change or add pictures. This refining process clarifies your dream and strengthens your resolve. It also is a good time to ask yourself some tough questions about your vision. I call them reality checks.

Reality Checks

As we learned in chapters 11 and 13, our vision needs to be linked to God's will if we want to have meaningful lives.

We have also talked in this book about the importance of being our authentic selves. Once you've put your vision on paper, it's wise to scrutinize it before you go any further. Ask yourself:

- Does my vision line up with God's will as revealed in the Bible?
- Can I ask God's blessing on my vision?
- Is this vision one that I could earnestly and prayerfully seek God's help with?
- Does this vision allow me to be myself?

If your vision is God-given, it will allow you to be true to yourself. The next thirty or forty years will not be fulfilling if you have to pretend to be someone you are not. Making changes at midlife does not mean turning into someone other than who you are. You want to release the real you so that your life will be happier and more fulfilling.

This stage of life is a time for your uniqueness to flourish—to let your creativity, your convictions, your values, your ideas, and your insights bloom. Being authentic doesn't mean you are perfect; it means not pretending to be perfect. It means admitting that you have weaknesses without sacrificing your self-worth. True authenticity also involves a greater awareness of others and a stronger desire for genuine relationships. It means being ready to pursue your own goals even if others ignore or oppose what is important to you, which is something Juanita learned.

The need for authenticity motivated Juanita to quit being her church's main cook. She was a superb organizer and a good cook, so naturally through the years her church leaned on her to organize various fellowship meals and banquets. When people complimented her, she would smile and say, "I'm a Martha." But in her heart she wanted to be Mary, the one who chose to sit at Jesus' feet (see Luke 10:38-42).

Juanita was in her mid-forties when her church asked her to be in charge of feeding five hundred youth who were coming to their church for a convention. She balked, saying to herself, *I simply cannot force myself to do this any longer.* The time and energy it took to plan and organize large meals could be given over to spiritual pursuits.

What Juanita wanted was to become involved in worship planning. In her conservative church where women held few leadership positions, this was going to be difficult, but Juanita was ready for the challenge. She said to me, "I can't stifle my true interests any longer."

Pam, whom you met at the beginning of this chapter, was in a church where she could implement her vision without much interference. Already an active member of her church and respected by church leaders, no one questioned her when she started organizing retreats. She was even able to handpick her assistants. Juanita was not so fortunate. When she told her pastor, "No, I will not be in charge of feeding five hundred youth at the convention," she shared with him her desire to be a part of the worship planning. He raised an eyebrow and said, "I appreciate your sharing that with me." What she longed for him to say was, "I welcome your help. When can we talk more about this?"

Later, when the convention was over, she went to him again. This time he said, "Planning the worship is something the staff does together. I think we can handle it. Maybe down the line you can help us with some special programs such as a Christmas service."

Eventually Juanita had to change churches to find one where the laity—including women—could be involved in worship planning. This took awhile, and at times she was tempted to be discouraged. That's when she remembered her vision: she had a hunger to serve the Lord, to be involved in worship planning, and to be her authentic self.

Juanita's experience reminds us of some more questions to answer as reality checks:

- What do I have to do and learn in order to see my vision become reality?
- Am I willing to make investments in learning and in lifestyle changes?
- What realistic changes will I have to make?
- Am I willing to make those changes?

For most of us, our dreams won't become reality unless we are committed to our vision and willing to make changes.

COMMITMENT

Your vision will act as your inner compass. As one woman expressed it, "[Our vision] keeps our ship sailing in the right direction." Possession of a dream, though, does not guarantee fulfilling that dream. Life has a way of eroding dreams. The demands and expectations of others also press in on us. Even our own good intentions may get left by the wayside unless we commit to seeing our vision become a reality. Putting your vision on paper increases your determination, helps you to evaluate it, and gives you a chance to see what it's going to take to make your dream become reality. Recording your vision on paper can also help you to develop specific goals and can provide guidelines to help you stay on track.

When I asked our discussion group members to write their goals for the next ten years, one of the participants balked. Overwhelmed by family and financial problems, she shrugged her shoulders and said, "What's the use?"

I understood. I had felt the same way for years. I avoided reading articles and attending workshops on the subject of goals because I didn't see myself as having choices. My life was wrapped up in being adaptable to the needs of others and keeping bills paid. Now I was determined to be one of God's spokeswomen, but that was a broad concept. If I wanted to be an encourager and a deliverer of God's messages, how was I going to do that? How would I measure whether I had succeeded?

My vision was short on specifics, but a sense of time running out forced me to make decisions, and I turned my dreams into goals. As I wrote them in my journal, I wrote the word R-E-S-O-L-V-E on my heart.

Nancy, another member of our group, whom you first met in chapter 4, also resisted thinking about new goals: "I worked hard to develop goals in the past and now they are accomplished. It's hard work to start fresh with all new goals." After thinking about it, Nancy understood why she was resistant to writing down her goals. She said, "When you state a goal in writing, it stands there, daring you to accomplish it." She's right. "People who write down their goals tend to reach them more often and sooner than people who do not. Putting a goal down on paper makes it more real, more attainable."[2]

Nancy's resistance faded as our discussion prompted her to think about her future. When she came to our last meeting, she proudly showed us her goals. She said, "My goals revolve around four words: Serve God and Learn. I know that God is asking me to serve: to guide my husband to God; to live a life so that my family will know God through my example; to mirror God's love to the larger community; to offer laughter as an example of God's love; to offer music as an example of God's love; to offer friendship as an example of God's love. I seek to create a more harmonious work environment. I seek freedom to give love to my husband as his needs dramatically change and to have the courage to guide my husband through the end of his life. I want to support and encourage my children and their spouses and to have significant relationships with my grandchildren. I want to surround myself in music and a creative environment. I want to receive recognition for my work, and I want to find time for myself." She bubbled with enthusiasm as she told us how she was doing: "In making decisions, I simply go back to this vision and see if the situation fits."

While writing your vision and/or goals strengthens your resolve, so does verbalizing your vision. I told my oldest son and my husband what my goals were. I knew that I would be more earnest about working on them if I did. While I doubt they would have held me accountable (as in, "I thought you were going to . . . "), I felt accountable anyway. Telling them my goals was a miniature commencement ceremony. I was beginning a new life.

Sharing your vision with close friends or family members also elicits their support and prayers—something we need in order to remain committed. Accountability and /or support groups are also helpful. We can form a group of women our age who want to pursue changes in their lives, or we can look for groups of people who are working on similar goals.

SURPRISED BY GROWTH

Even with 100 percent effort and commitment, we cannot guarantee that our dreams will come true. We do not control all the variables. But the pursuit alone brings energy and vitality to the way we live. The pursuit is just as important as the result.

When I attended my first NSA meeting, a seasoned speaker took me aside, asked my age, and said, "You need to know that speaking is a very competitive business—very competitive." He could have saved his breath. I had done enough speaking already to know that. Writing is also very competitive. The likelihood that I would fail was great. Since then, I've made blunders and embarrassed myself, but I'm growing, and it's exhilarating. By the standards of others, I still may not be a success, but I can't remember a time in my life when I've felt more fully alive.

From time to time, I go back and look at my written goals. Like a child putting a notch on the doorframe to see how tall she has grown, I take note of how I've grown. I've almost succeeded in accomplishing my first set of goals, and I have learned so much. I've learned about myself and I'm seeing my strengths and weaknesses more clearly. I've learned much about speaking and writing. God is opening my eyes in so many ways, and I'm asking Him now what He wants me to aim for next. I anticipate this unfolding process to repeat itself over and over as the years go by. Always a vision out in front, always growing.

You may be hesitant to follow your dreams because you don't have the necessary skills and knowledge, but returning to school can bring an aliveness to your life. Maybe that aliveness is why so many middle-aged adults want to learn; maybe they're hooked on the feeling that comes with it. Even when you're striving, stumbling, and struggling, it's exhilarating if you sense that you're growing.

You may be frightened to do some of the things you have to do in order to see your dream become a reality, but that will prompt you to reach out for God's help. Your faith will be exercised and you will grow spiritually.

Remember: The final result is *not* what is important. What's important are these considerations: Do you have a dream? Are you committed to that dream? Can you be true to yourself if you follow the dream? Will you feel fully alive as you strive to reach your potential? Will you grow in the process?

PART THREE

EMBRACING ALL THAT GOD HAS FOR YOU

CHAPTER FIFTEEN

WISDOM PLUS

What Does It Mean to Follow Christ at My Age?

In my twenties, I could work on a drama for church until midnight or later, night after night, and still be fresh at work the next day. There is no way I could do that now. But the tradeoff is that today I have the maturity to mentor younger people, who bring their energy to the church program. I can encourage, help finance, and share the wisdom of my stories with them. I didn't lose my edge by aging; my slant simply changed.[1]

MARLENE LEFEVER, AFTER TURNING FIFTY

I RECENTLY LOANED THE BOOK *WOMEN AS RISK-TAKERS FOR GOD* to a thirty-year-old in my church. When Donna returned it, she raved about the stories of dynamic women who dared to exercise their spiritual gifts. Her response was just what I hoped it would be. Then she said, "I didn't know women past forty could have such powerful spiritual lives."

A bit taken aback, I asked her to explain.

She said, "It's been my observation that after age forty, adults just sit."

As the furrows in my brow deepened, she said, "I don't know . . . I guess I got this impression when I was in high school. Our youth group would go away for mission trips and come back so excited for the Lord. We always hoped our excitement would spread to the adults, but it never did."

Within a few days of this conversation, I was involved in two other conversations that had a similar thread. One was with Marie, a friend from another church. Her church was without a pastor. An evangelist had been brought in for a special meeting. Bubbling with enthusiasm, Marie said, "I wish we could have him as our pastor. He's *young* and dynamic—just what our church needs."

The other conversation was with Joyce. While waiting in line at the post office, she said, "I've just been to a retreat in Nashville. It was great."

Always interested in successful retreats, I said, "What made it great?"

"You could really feel the Spirit's presence."

"Why do you think that was?"

"There were so many *young* women there."

Now, I know that three conversations do not a statistic make, but I'll admit I've heard comments like these throughout my adult life. Their subtle effect is that we associate spiritual fervency with the young. Currently on my desk is a missions magazine with an article titled "For Real *Passion,* Look to the Young."

Earlier in this book, I noted that we live in a culture that worships youth. Some of us attend churches that come close to doing the same thing, so much so that the work of the Holy Spirit is often associated with a youthful spirit. Perhaps it is their enthusiasm fueled by their vigor and idealism that causes us to make this connection. But if we midlife women buy into this attitude, we may assume that our prime time for serving the Lord has passed. We may assume that no one past forty has a spiritually dynamic life. And what's worse, some of us may not care.

What We've Lost

About the time her children began leaving home, Vida felt she had already done enough in the church. She was tired of working in Vacation Bible School, helping with church dinners, and teaching Sunday school. Now when she's asked to serve, she feels a sense of *I've done that already* and doesn't want to do it again.

Marilyn works a forty-hour week that requires an hour commute one way. She's also taking classes to keep up with the educational requirements of her job. Every Friday night and all day Saturday she baby-sits her granddaughters. On Sunday morning she enters the worship service late and quickly exits when it's over because she's afraid someone will approach her about getting involved. For that, she just doesn't have time.

When we were young, we had a fresh, confident, God-can-do-anything, all-will-turn-out-well kind of faith. In chapter 12 we noted that our faith at midlife may be more realistic because the stresses and strains of life have tempered it. We aren't without faith, but we may conclude that we have an inferior faith because our faith doesn't "feel" like the idealistic faith we once had. Or perhaps we think we don't have the energy for a dynamic spiritual life. Supposing that we accept all of this as just part and parcel of growing older, will it matter?

It does matter if we want to continue to grow, especially to grow spiritually. In chapters 9, 11, 12, and 13, we learned that the spiritually fulfilled life calls for doing what God wants. When the crowd asked Jesus, "What can we do in order to do what God wants us to do?" Jesus answered, "What God wants you to do is to believe in the one he sent" (John 6:28-29, TEV).

This is no academic belief; it calls for action. To believe that Jesus is real is to follow Him. We knew how to follow Christ as young adults. Unencumbered with possessions, we could readily go wherever God was leading. We could serve energetically. Our idealism made it easier to believe we could change the world. There were fewer "Yes . . . but" variables to serving the Lord. But now that our energy has lessened, our lives are fuller, and our faith is tempered, what does it mean to follow Christ?

Look at What We've Gained

We may not have youthful vigor or youth's idealism, but we have wisdom. This is not to say that all midlife women are wise, but neither are all youth vigorous and idealistic. Wisdom, as we noted in chapter 9, was a trait that survey respondents associated with women over forty-five, and it was repeatedly referred to (as if it were a given) in much of the literature I read about midlife women.

The book of Proverbs encourages us to seek wisdom at any age, and young King Solomon asked for and received wisdom as a gift from God to rule his people (see 1 Kings 3:5-14). But there is also wisdom that comes with aging. Don't you know things now that you didn't know when you were younger? Don't you have insight because of what you have seen and experienced? At times I'm tempted to agree with Erik Erikson's belief: "Lots of old people don't get wise, but you don't get wise unless you age."[2]

The self-evaluation struggle we go through in middlescence may lead us to see that we are wise. We may not all be wise in the same areas or about the same things, but we have the gift of wisdom that comes with aging. How can we use it? The Bible shows us three examples of biblical women who used their wisdom to help people.

Deborah, whose story is told in Judges 4 and 5, was obedient to God's covenant while many of God's people were disobedient. Recognizing her wisdom, people came to her to have their disputes settled (see Judges 4:5). The Bible describes Deborah as "the one who was responsible for bringing the people back to God" (4:4, TLB). Imagine God saying that of you! What's even more amazing is that Deborah had this level of influence in a culture that viewed women as inferior to men, and yet even men came to her in her role as a judge.

Naomi lived about the same time as Deborah. When Naomi and her daughter-in-law Ruth returned to Bethlehem after living in Moab, they were penniless widows. So that she and Naomi could survive, Ruth went to the barley fields and gathered grain left behind by the harvesters (see Ruth 2:2-3). When Ruth came home, telling how the owner of the fields, Boaz, was nice to her, Naomi brightened (see 2:17-20). She instructed Ruth on what to do to get Boaz to marry her (see 3:1-5). Ruth complied (what a daughter-in-law!), and the widows survived. Ruth and Boaz married, and Naomi gained a grandchild.

Naomi was practical; she knew what it would take to survive in the culture and she made a plan to do so. As midlife women, we have practical wisdom that others could benefit from. We've raised children, balanced budgets, cut corners, met deadlines and quotas, and planned fund-raisers. I have a lot of practical wisdom if someone would just ask.

I remember one church I was in where the younger women were discussing "what to fix" for their families. I rattled off a few of my menus. One of them asked, "Do you plan your meals ahead of time?"

"Yes, I do. I keep them in a notebook."

Another woman asked, "Could we see your menus?"

I took them to the next meeting and they read them over, asked me questions, photocopied them, and took them home. I was thrilled! No one had ever asked to see my menus before—and haven't since. I have a lot more practical wisdom tucked away inside me. I think other women do too. The problem isn't a lack of wisdom as much as it is finding an avenue for sharing it—something we'll learn more about in the next two chapters.

Another wise woman in the Bible is the mother of King Lemuel (see Proverbs 31:1). We are more familiar with what she said than who she was. Her description of the virtuous woman (Proverbs 31:10-31) is a much-quoted section of the Bible. She described this woman to her son as the kind of woman she wanted him to marry. Lemuel's mother stands in stark contrast to the father figure who gave instructions to a son in many passages of

Proverbs. He cautioned the son against wicked women; Lemuel's mother offered a very positive view of a woman. Her well-rounded description reflects her wisdom, and men and women have been quoting her ever since.

Wisdom enables women to be leaders, problem-solvers, and advisers. By itself, wisdom can lead to spiritual power, but it grows in power if combined with other strengths such as integrity, people skills, compassion, and independence.

WISDOM +

In his book *Integrity,* Stephen L. Carter says you can't be a person of integrity unless you have gone through a sorting out process.[3] By the time we are forty-five, many of us have "sorted out" our lives. We have wrestled with temptation, we have experienced the consequences of our actions, and we have observed life. We know what we believe. The combination of wisdom and integrity gives us the courage to speak out on controversial issues, the security to be a dependable rock for young people, and the conviction to be activists for social, moral, and spiritual causes.

If we combine wisdom, integrity, and people skills, we are especially suited for positions of authority: matriarchal roles in the home and family, leadership positions in the church and community, and management opportunities in the workplace.

Wisdom, integrity, and people skills make a wonderful spiritual mix; if we want the mix to be even more flavorful, we can toss in the spice of independence. How many times in your young adult years did you hesitate to witness because you were afraid of being rejected? How many times did you tolerate a wrong or avoid controversy because you were afraid of not being liked? A woman gains spiritual power when she's not so concerned with what people think.

GIVING THE SOUL A REST

Some women I've talked with—especially those who have been involved in leadership activities—want a more reflective spiritual journey at midlife. That's fine too. Like the widow Anna, they want to spend their days and nights worshiping God, fasting, and praying (see Luke 2:36-37). Outside of following God's general principles, such as those found in the Ten Commandments and Jesus' teachings, there is nothing in the Bible that says we have to follow Christ in the same way throughout our lives. In fact, we may want to take a spiritual sabbatical to sort out all of this.

The Bible speaks of the fiftieth year as the year of Jubilee. "Consecrate the fiftieth year and proclaim liberty throughout the land to all its inhabitants. It shall be a jubilee for you; each one of you is to return to his family property and each to his own clan. The fiftieth year shall be a jubilee for you; do not sow and do not reap. . . . For it is a jubilee and is to be holy for you" (Leviticus 25:10-12).

Of course, the passage refers to giving the land a rest, but sometimes we need to rest our souls. We may need to cease from our activism—the sowing and the reaping—for a period of time. We may need to return to the roots of our personal faith if we want spiritual power. Where have we come from? What is important? For what do we truly hunger and thirst?

We may need to make time for spiritual contemplation about what is next. If we've been teaching Sunday school for twenty years, maybe it's time to do something else. If we have been quiet learners, maybe it's time we volunteered to teach. If we've been on a nonstop career track, maybe we need a spiritual break to reclaim our soul. Maybe we want to change arenas and use our expertise and skills to leave this world a better place instead of focusing on profit.

A spiritual sabbatical will renew our spirits and strengthen our resolve to serve in ways that fit who we are and what we have to give at this time in our lives. Our passion for serving Christ will return when we know where we've come from and where we're going.

Faith for Following

The church needs the energetic and optimistic perspective of youth, and it needs the mature perspective that can come with age. I've been in churches where we didn't have grandparents, and I've been in churches where we had too many grandparents. The churches full of young adults sometimes made rash decisions in the name of faith; those full of older adults were sometimes stagnant and complacent. God's power is not found in complacent faith or blind faith; it is found in the "becoming faith" we talked about in chapter 12.

Saundra, whom you met in chapters 1 and 11, said: "The trust we have now will not be an innocent, untested kind of trust, like when we first believed. At this age, we look back over our lives and acknowledge God's faithfulness to us in all the good times, hard times, agonizing times, and times that we still don't understand. We grab all those times up in our arms so that we can lay them at the feet of Christ. He receives them, gathers them up, and creates a practical walking stick out of them. If we choose to pick up that walking stick and keep following Him, in glory that walking stick will turn into a crown we can lay at His feet and praise Him with forever."

THE ADVENTURE OF FOLLOWING

By using our wisdom and other assets we've gained by this age, we can be spiritually strong without having youthful vigor and idealism. But we do need a tinge of another quality that many young people possess: a willingness to risk. The young have a sense of invulnerability that causes them to be adventuresome and to take risks, sometimes tragically so. We've lived long enough to know that we can be hurt and we can fail, and some of us react by becoming too security conscious. For a long time, Bea has known she needs to make a career change, but that would probably mean moving to another state. She resists and puts it off because she doesn't want to move. The major reason? She doesn't want to leave the fantastic Christian medical professionals in her area.

In contrast, Sadie made a leap of faith. In her survey, she wrote, "I worked for a chamber of commerce in my city for almost ten years. I prayed for personnel changes in staff but I knew the Lord wanted me to move on. I had no other job at the time but followed God's lead, and I've never regretted it."

Health and security are two major concerns of midlife

women; but when we become overly concerned, our faith stagnates. Unless we are willing to take some risk, we're limiting what God can do in our lives. I'm not recommending tossing out good judgment, but a healthy faith needs a sense of adventure. We are on a pilgrimage, and we shouldn't want to miss out on the new experiences God may have for us because we want to always be safe and secure.

"Some people are scared of anything that doesn't have a certain end and all the risk removed. We seek a smooth path, without any brambles or stones in the way, a straight way without too much incline that leads us to heaven quite safely. On the other hand, God, the great Adventurer, leads us over high peaks, across rocky crags, up steep ravines, across rivers we thought we couldn't cross, and gets us to heaven all breathless, bearing the fruit of our effort and the likeness of His Son—and fit for royal fellowship."[4]

One woman told me, "I face the challenge of using my God-given power." We all do if we want to follow Christ. We may not have the energy of youth but we can have an invigorating Christian life if we recognize our strengths, use the faith we have, and are willing to take risks. All that has gone before has been an elaborate preparation for what we can do now and for what we can now become.

CHAPTER SIXTEEN

A TOUCH OF ME

How Can I Leave My Mark on This World?

Realizing I have more life behind me than in front of me, what kind of person I present to the Lord and what influence I leave behind are of utmost importance to me.

DONNA, A SURVEY PARTICIPANT

AT MY FIRST DISCUSSION GROUP WITH MIDLIFE WOMEN, I ASKED them, "What kind of spiritual questions are you asking?" Before I could elaborate, Jane—a perky, vivacious woman—said, "Have I made an impact?"

During middlescence, we begin wondering, When I am gone, will anyone know I have been here? Will my life have counted? How will I be remembered? Will I have made a difference? Leaving a legacy—making an impact—is important to us.

In this book I've used the word "vision" to refer to the mental image we have of who we can be and what we can do, and I've used the words "purpose" and "impact" to describe our eternal significance. In other words, purpose answers the question, *What's the point of my being here?* Impact, though, is thinking about what we are going to leave behind. We want to produce something that will outlive us.

For some of us, our vision, purpose, and impact will be inseparable. From the beginning, when we started building our dream for the future, we wanted a purposeful life in which we could influence others in a lasting way. For others of us, the desire to make an impact springs up alongside what we are doing. It may be a by-product or it may be something altogether separate. For example, my vision, as you know by now, is to be one of God's spokeswomen. I'll confess that when I was defining my dream, I never gave any thought to leaving a legacy. I was thinking about getting to be me and using the gifts God gave me. Maybe something I say or write will have an impact, but when I'm thinking of making a lasting contribution, my thoughts turn toward my sons. That's where I want to make my impact. I want my epitaph to read, "Her children arise and call her blessed" (Proverbs 31:28).

If I correctly understand the literature on adult development, this desire to leave a legacy is something most people experience as they age. Maybe it has to do with seeing life as a gift that is coming to an end. Will anyone know I've walked this way? Or, maybe it has to do with the freedom we've found away from young adult expectations and pressures. We get involved because we want to, not because we have to or ought to. Responding to this urge not only leaves our mark on the world, but it also increases our sense of well-being and helps us avoid becoming self-absorbed and stagnant.

When Pat, the retired school administrator mentioned in chapter 5, saw the question on making an impact, she said, "I don't think we have any control over that." Well, I believe we do. Sometimes all we need is our consciousness raised about how we can do it, so let me share with you some of the ways that midlife women want to make an impact.

Telling Others About Christ

Many respondents wanted to make an impact by telling others about Jesus.

- "I want to be an example to others around me of what Christ is like so they can see Him as He is and grow closer to Him."
- "I have a real burden for those who don't yet know Christ. I want to share Him with others."
- "I want to let women know they can have an inner peace through a personal relationship with Jesus Christ."

Jesus' departing words to His followers included "be my witnesses in Jerusalem, and in all Judea and Samaria, and to the ends of the earth" (Acts 1:8). For much of our lives, many of us have witnessed in our Jerusalem—in our immediate area where we live. But midlife may mean more money available for travel, or more free time, allowing us the opportunity to go to foreign lands to share the gospel.

That's what these two women did:

- "If God allows me to, I pray I will be able to go back to Ukraine and work with the people I love so much. I want to be a part of what God is doing in that country. I want to help strengthen churches there and encourage Christians."

- "Since I participated in a missionary trip to Ukraine two years ago, I have committed myself to pray daily for them and to try to help a family come to the United States. I am committed to helping them financially and spiritually. I hope to be a great encouragement to them."

These women have captured the spirit of the psalmist who prayed, "Even when I am old and gray, do not forsake me, O God, till I declare your power to the next generation, your might to all who are to come" (Psalm 71:18).

INVESTING IN CHILDREN AND GRANDCHILDREN

When talk centers on leaving a legacy, the thoughts of many turn toward home—to their children and/or grandchildren. As one respondent said, "I want to be a positive role model for my family." Some midlife women have children still at home; others have children in the process of leaving home or out on their own. While their children are living at home, they, of course, hope to make an impact, but that hope continues to flourish even when the children are on their own.

- "I want to support in prayer, communication, and encouragement my children's endeavors toward independence."
- "I want to encourage my adult children as a friend."

As this last statement indicates, we may have to change our approach if we want to continue to influence our adult children. I've learned the truth of that the hard way through being a little too generous with my wisdom!

Many survey respondents touted the joys of being a grandparent, and this is where they want to leave their mark.

- "I want to be a positive influence on my grandchildren."
- "I want to have an impact in the lives of my grandchildren."
- "I want to keep in touch by phone and mail with my grandtwins and visit them three to four times a year."
- "I want to be a godly grandma."

- "I want to be a good example for them to follow as they grow and mature. I want them to see Jesus and His love in me."
- "We just took our granddaughter to college. Without our help, she wouldn't be able to afford to go. I feel very strongly about 'being there' to help her, to encourage her, or do whatever she needs. She wouldn't have a chance otherwise, and she's very important to us."

We can impact the lives of our grandchildren by sharing our family's history, passing on values, introducing them to Jesus, encouraging them, listening to them, praying for them, and being there for them.

Nurturing Children

Not all women have children and/or grandchildren. When feelings of generativity begin to tug at them, latent maternal instincts may surface. Martha was single and working in health care management when she heard of a program that involved rocking babies at a hospital. Even though she wasn't a kid-person, she decided to volunteer. She focused on rocking HIV-positive babies. Within days she was under the spell of the tiny, love-starved bundles. She took home a three-month-old infant as a foster child; within a few months she had taken home five more. Today, in her late forties, Martha is the full-time mother to eight children. One of the children has AIDS, another has cerebral palsy, and several have emotional problems. Martha says, "People tell me these kids are lucky to have me, but I feel I'm lucky to have them."

Sally wasn't a kid-person either, but after a missions trip to the Philippines, she decided to host exchange students in her home. Each school year she mothers a new daughter. Sally and her husband are able to nurture the lives of these young women, helping them to mature and introducing them to Jesus. One by one, they are making an impact on one young woman after another. Sally said, "It is so much fun having these girls in our home. I just can't believe how much I enjoy it. It adds a whole new dimension to my life. If it's up to me, I'll never go another year without a student."

MENTORING OTHER WOMEN

Denise wrote, "I have had so much joy from sharing my faith with the younger women I've worked with. My role has been a nurturing one, and it's a thrill to see their interest grow in knowing and serving the Lord." Patsy said, "I have begun mentoring young women in one-on-one situations. I have found this to be very rewarding, and I'm learning so much from them." Denise and Patsy are living the principle exemplified in the apostle Paul's writing to Titus.

Paul told Titus what he should teach and how he should apply it to various groups within the congregation he was pastoring (see Titus 2). Paul's specific instructions for the older women were to teach and train the younger women (see Titus 2:3-5).

When we looked at this passage in our discussion group, several women remarked they had not thought of themselves as the "older women." Isn't that the way it is? Whoever is old, there's always someone older than we are! Considering what the life span would have been in Paul's day, the older women would be our age. And whether or not we identify with the label, we are older to younger women. If you don't know this already, you'll realize it the first time a seventeen-year-old waitress offers you a senior citizen discount!

This teaching and training of younger women can take on many forms. It might take place in a class or it might be through friendships or small groups. It may be part of a mentoring relationship or a discipleship relationship.

Some churches and/or women's ministries have ministries organized around the Titus 2 concept. Parachurch organizations also encourage and assist in this. Some individual women see it as a biblical basis for organizing such ministries. Deborah opened a ministry for the emotional and spiritual healing of hurting women in her community. At fifty-two, Reova, whom you met in chapter 13, left her secure teaching job three years short of receiving full retirement pay and started a center for ministering to women. Women volunteers help other women cope with abuse, divorce, death, eating disorders, fears and phobias, incarceration, parenting issues, spirituality, pregnancy, relationships, sexuality, and thoughts of suicide. In addition to counseling, services include support groups, prayer groups, and Bible studies. All of this is done in a nonjudgmental environment without a fee.

Casey joined two mentoring programs, one at her church and one at the local women's pregnancy center where she volunteers weekly. Rita didn't respond to organized approaches because she wanted to spend the time mentoring her daughters who are in various stages of leaving home, going to college, getting married, and starting their families. She wanted to be available to help them with their transitions, to teach them about baby care and housecleaning. It was a joy to be able to pass on to her daughters specific instructions about homemaking.

Geraldine didn't opt for the organized approach either. She was trying to finish her college degree and didn't have the time to participate in her church's Titus 2 program. When she came upon a discouraged nineteen-year-old who was crying in the women's lounge one day, she realized she could be a Titus 2 woman to the younger women on campus. This enhanced her college experience because she felt like she had a ministry as well as an opportunity to learn.

Some of us may immediately be drawn to the specific areas Paul mentioned for training younger women: to love their husbands and children, to be self-controlled and pure, to be busy at home, to be kind, and to be subject to their husbands (see Titus 2:5). Lynn wrote, "I feel a real burden right now to share with young parents the importance of spiritual training in the home!"

Others may be ill at ease about some of these areas. I don't think I could train younger women in self-control (I'm still working on that!), but Jo has the right credentials. She is the survey respondent quoted in chapter 5 who lost over one hundred pounds. With God's help, she kept it off and has become an encourager to younger women. "Today I'm very grateful and humble and I work daily to keep my focus. With this, I encourage others, using my testimony, to help those who struggle with major health problems."

We all have something to give because we are women of wisdom and experience. As Susan Hunt wrote in *Spiritual Mothering,* Paul's "command is in no way intended to be an exhaustive statement about the role of woman,"[1] and I agree. Older women have strengths to share with younger women. In today's world, young women are facing all kinds of pressures, struggling with stress and temptations. We who have come through those trials have much to give them. Young adults are so afraid of failing. We know we can fail and still survive.

Regardless of whether you feel called by God to be a Titus 2 woman, you can be a role model. You can leave your mark by the way you care for your invalid parents, by the way you handle yourself on the job, or by the way you take on new challenges. The important thing is that you have a sense of being an example to younger women.

TELLING OUR STORIES

Kathleen wrote, "If I could just get a manuscript published, I would feel that I had made an important contribution to the lives of others. I want to write because I have some good stories in my head." Don't we all have stories? By the time we are forty-five, we've experienced a lot and seen a lot. Stories are swirling around in our heads and in our hearts. Sharing those stories in writing can be a wonderful way to leave our mark.

Judy started writing in her late forties. She said, "For the first time I really looked at and pursued my heart's deepest interests and desires. This resulted in following my heart's path and writing a book." In her book *Something of Your Own,* Judy used her story to help women discover and follow their dreams.

While it gives me pleasure to know that some of the books I've written are in seminary libraries where students can use them for years to come, I don't think a person has to be published in order to leave a legacy of words. We can write our stories for family and friends, just as Jessie Lee Brown Foveaux. At the age of eighty, Jessie attended a program for senior citizens where a teacher asked them to write stories about growing up. Reluctant, but too polite to refuse, she wrote about her childhood, about her life of rearing eight children, about struggling with an alcoholic husband, and things that just struck her fancy.[2]

Once she started writing, Jessie couldn't quit. She filled up notebook after notebook. She wanted to leave her children and grandchildren something aside from scrapbooks and some Fred Waring albums. She hoped they might find her writings useful, and they did.[3] For example, in her writings she explained why she never spoke of her late husband and why she left the room when his name was mentioned and why he was absent from family photos lining her shelves. Her children, who both loved and feared their father, could now understand things they never had before. One of her children said, "As children, you don't ask questions; but as you grow older, you want to know."

We have stories to tell—family history, personal history, and spiritual history. We can put those stories on paper. We can let our grandchildren or children know what is important to us. We can let them know how we arrived at the decisions we did. We can let them know our convictions and why we believe the way we do. We can make an impact through words.

How Can I Leave My Mark?

These roles certainly reflect our desire for and our interest in relationships, but our other strengths also lend themselves to making an impact. For example, we can use our wisdom and independence to take action. This is what Joan did. When she was fifty-four, she was hired as a part-time instructor and part-time adviser at a technical college. She wrote, "What I had was two part-time jobs at an hourly wage, and a low one at that. Part-timers were not represented by a union as were the well-paid full-timers." She was determined to begin a grass-roots organization to unionize the part-timers. Over the next three years she contacted 1,200 part-timers, distributed flyers, organized meetings, and talked with union representatives. Through her leadership, the part-timers gained representation, and the union will go on helping part-timers for years to come.

By exploring the question, "How can I leave my mark?" we have opened our eyes to various possibilities. There are many more possibilities besides those mentioned in this chapter. For women of purpose, at peace with ourselves and with God, the possibilities are endless. We have the power to make a difference.

CHAPTER SEVENTEEN

DREAM-SHARING

How Can I Help Others Understand the New Me?

"This is the best time of my life. I love being old." At that point a voice from the audience asked loudly, "Why is it good to be old?" I answered spontaneously . . . , "because I am more myself than I have ever been. There is less conflict. I am happier, more balanced, and" (I heard myself say rather aggressively) "more powerful." I felt it was rather an odd word "powerful," but I think it is true. It might have been more accurate to say "I am better able to use my powers."[1]

May Sarton at Hartford College in Connecticut

MIDDLESCENCE, THAT PASSAGE BETWEEN YOUNG ADULTHOOD and middle adulthood, begins with inner discontent, hazy fears, nagging questions, disturbing dreams, and a sense that the old pattern no longer fits. Darlene described it this way: "It's as if your life is a scratchy wool sweater that doesn't quite fit anymore and makes you itch."

Middlescence ends when we're ready to embrace the middle years and the person we have envisioned becoming. Or, to put it in Darlene's terms, the scratchy wool sweater is replaced by cashmere. The size and the color of the new sweater are just right, and its softness makes it comfortable. You have a new belief in yourself because you went through an exploration process. You changed, even if your world didn't. Old images and expectations may still be around to pull and tug on your cashmere sweater.

THE PRESSURE OF EXPECTATIONS

Earlier we discussed how our culture and sometimes our families and churches have images of who a middle-aged woman is and what she should do. While we were changing, these images probably did not. Some of our family members and some of our friends may not appreciate our inaccessibility when we actively pursue our goals. They may resent our attention to other pursuits.

A writer of children's books worked at home where she was always available for her children. Whenever they wanted or needed something, she always dropped what she was doing to respond. As her children left home, she decided to tackle researching and writing on intimacy among adults. She became engrossed in the research. One day when her youngest son was home from college for the weekend, he came into her office and asked her to sew a button on his shirt. Although she didn't say a word as she reached for her sewing basket, her look said, "You want me to stop what I'm doing and sew this button on *now?*" He said to her, "I have never seen that look in your eyes before, and I don't like it."

Our loved ones may grumble because of the way our changes affect them. Filled with vision and empowered, we may be bursting with energy. We may be thinking, *Hey, I've got thirty to forty years ahead of me!* while our husbands or friends are saying, "I'm ready to slow down." They may not approve of the new woman; they may even want the former woman to return.

Others, too, may have expectations that inhibit us. Our capabilities may be underutilized and underappreciated because we're automatically stereotyped. For example, an employer may want to hire someone younger because he views younger people as more flexible and trainable.

Many young people view middle-agers and older people the same way they view McDonald's. They know what the menu is so they drive right on by; nothing new or interesting there, which makes a relationship connection difficult.

The Gap

I heard that Ellen had started a group for young women in her church. That puzzled me because I knew the church already had a strong women's organization. When I saw Ellen in the grocery store, I asked her about it. She said, "Well, I just felt like we needed our own organization. After all, what do we have in common with older women?"

"Did they not deal with any of your needs at their meetings?" I asked.

"Well, I don't really know because I never attended any of their meetings. They are into missions and crafts. We're into children and marriage. They wouldn't understand our needs."

I'm all for Elizabeth-Mary groups where women with similar interests get together to support one another. Elizabeth and Mary shared their time of pregnancy together, and it's healthy for women to do that. But what bothered me was Ellen's assumption that older women would not understand, as if they knew nothing about marriage or children.

This conversation made me hesitant about approaching a

young woman whom I wanted to mentor. Heather's husband was often gone, and she spent many hours alone with preschoolers. Her life reminded me of mine when my first two sons were preschoolers and my husband was a busy graduate student. I thought I might be able to encourage her. I decided to test the waters by asking, "Heather, how do you feel about Titus 2 women? You know the concept, older women in the church teaching younger women?" She responded, "I don't want anybody telling me what to do. I've read all the books—James Dobson's and all the others. I know what I am supposed to do."

As I left her house, I was reminded of a line from Letty Cottin Pogrebin's book *Getting Over Getting Older*: "Middle age is when you finally have all the answers, but nobody will ask you the questions."[2]

Even if we encounter resistance, that doesn't mean we should second-guess ourselves or give up our vision. Problems and limitations naturally crop up when we commit to being the person God wants us to be. At the same time, we don't want to alienate others by our pursuit. Fulfilling our dream is important, but so is living in harmony. Besides, we also need the support and cooperation of others if we are going to succeed. What can we do? How can we help others understand who we are?

SHARE YOUR DREAMS

Frances Weaver, author of *The Girls with the Grandmother Faces,* wrote, "It's important to understand each other's motives in a family."[3] I think that goes for friendships as well. Our family members and friends are not mind readers. They won't know what is going on in our minds and hearts unless we tell them.

Weaver, a widow, asked her children's permission when she decided to move from Colorado to upstate New York to go to college.[4] She also insisted that each of her children and their spouses visit the college and check it out. She didn't have to ask for permission, but she did. She said, "What I *did* need was their approval, for my own peace of mind."[5] Weaver's approach encouraged dialogue and helped her family members to catch her vision and excitement.

When we share our vision, we can't expect to say it just once and then everybody cheers and waves us on to do our thing. If we want their cooperation and support, some negotiation, and some education and reassuring, may be required.

What we choose to do will have ramifications. A series of talks may be needed to work these out to everyone's satisfaction. When Roxie wanted the challenge of selling financial services instead of Tupperware, her husband balked. She later said, "My husband didn't want me to work myself to death. He wanted me to slow down. We spent many hours negotiating ground rules and a new division of chores. I had stayed home with the kids while they were growing up; now I asked my husband to give me five years, then I would slow down. He said okay."

Once your have shared your vision, and your family members or friends seem to understand, they may still expect the same things you used to provide for them. Old habits die hard, so we have to educate others about our new roles. Frequently I have had to remind my husband that I'm not available in the way I once was. Bob is a generous, caring person and proud of my cooking, so through the years he's made many spontaneous promises of casseroles and soups to people in need, knowing that I would come through. While I would still like to do that, I don't always have the time. When Bob forgets, I gently remind him, "I will do it this time if you will chop the vegetables, but please do not volunteer me again without checking with me first. Remember, I don't have as much time now as I used to."

I'm fortunate that my husband understands the value of pursuing dreams; not all wives are that lucky. As Peggy, the counselor you met earlier, noted, "For some men, a wife's goals may be a threat to their security, and it's definitely a threat to the comfortable way to which they've become accustomed. Many men enjoy having the lives of their wives and families revolve around them. When a wife begins pursuing her dreams, a man's life will change, and any change is often perceived as negative at first."

When husbands, friends, or children are threatened by our goals, we can continually reassure them of how important they are to us. We can say, "At this time in my life, I need your help. I will be able to love you better and more strongly when I am able to pursue my goals. You are very important to me and so are my dreams."

USE WINNING WAYS

When I was giving a talk, I shared the content of my conversation with Heather. Afterward, a woman about Heather's age came up to me and said, "You need to go back to Heather and try again. Be encouraging and let her know you won't be judgmental. We're afraid of people being critical of what we do and judging us. She needs to know you won't be like that." In other words, I needed to develop some winning ways.

According to Susan Hunt, author of *Spiritual Mothering,* if we want to be Titus 2 women, we need to develop nurturing relationships through being affirming, encouraging, and approachable.[6] In a warm, friendly manner, we can let others know who we are. We can let them see our individuality, and we can be interested in their lives. We need to take the first, second, or even third step to develop relationships. Out of those relationships, opportunities to mentor will grow.

Employers, just like our friends and family members, are not mind readers. I read about an organization that gave help to older women who had never been employed and were looking for jobs. One of the problems the organization had was getting the women to smile. We need to have winning ways when we're looking for jobs or changing jobs. By our smile, by our enthusiasm, by our interest in the business, by our confidence, we can help employers know who we are and what we're capable of.

Some of us may emerge from middlescence as strong, outspoken women. Our knowledge, if not used wisely, may turn off young people who want to make their own mistakes. We may say things that will shock others or make them uncomfortable. At times we may feel amused by this response, but if achieving our dreams or making an impact depends on working with and through an organization, church, or business, we will need to be concerned about how others react to us. Good leaders use tact when approaching others with their vision.

Let me add a caution: Even when we share our vision and use winning ways, not everyone will be convinced that we have chosen the right path. Jolene discovered this when she withdrew from her many church activities to develop a deeper spiritual life. Some of her fellow church members accused her by saying, "You are not doing your part." Jolene tried to explain to those she knew well, but still some of them did not understand. We can eliminate some resistance, but not all.

If we have a vision for our middle years of who we can be and what we can do, we have to be willing to accept being misunderstood. The resistance we experience may discourage us. For that reason, I recommend an accountability support group.

Help from Our Sisters

The February 1998 issue of *Ladies' Home Journal* reported that midlife discussion groups are currently hot.[7] I wonder if that isn't because baby boomers are discovering they need to talk with others about the changes they're experiencing. In groups of two, three, five, or eight, we can support and encourage each other, find solutions to our problems, and hold each other accountable.

Support. After I held several discussion groups, the daughter of one of the participants wrote to me. She said, "My mother really enjoyed meeting with your group, and I just wanted to let you know the positive impact it had on her. She has gone through so many changes in the past five years. It was good for her to express how she feels. She needs women her age who understand her."

Encouragement. We can talk over what bothers us with other women who are going through similar struggles. For example, if to follow her dream, a woman breaks up her family's regular pattern too drastically, she may experience guilt. Many of us have been programmed to support everyone else in our families, so it feels wrong to spend time and resources on ourselves. This happened to one discussion participant. She said, "Considering my personal potential can seem like an exercise in selfishness to me; but when I'm confronted by others who can see potential possibilities for me to use the gifts God has given me, plus my wisdom, I'm encouraged. This process gave me a vision for the future that I probably would never have been able to see for myself."

Problem-Solving. Our insights are always limited. But the resources of others can help us to see possibilities we are unaware of. When we're misunderstood at home, at work, at church, or in our social circles, we can talk about it with other women who understand our situation. Together we can brainstorm and find creative solutions.

Accountability. Cindy said, "I believe God gave me a glimpse of my personal potential, but sharing that glimpse with others who know me well gives me the confidence and motivation to go for it. I know when I go back to my growth group, they're going to ask, How's it going? Are you making progress? Are you on target? I want to be ready with a positive report."

From someone who was scared to reach her fiftieth birthday and beyond, I've become a cheerleader for midlife women. There's such energy, power, and wisdom present when we meet together. When we exchange ideas, talk about our goals, and pray together, we don't allow ourselves to be victimized by aging. We refuse to feel devalued, and we go on to gain the courage to confront our culture and resist conforming to expectations that might limit us. We encourage each other to pursue our visions. It's cashmere we're wearing now, and it feels just right!

CHAPTER EIGHTEEN

THE URGE TO SURGE

Now That I Have Answers . . .

I went to the woods because I wished to live deliberately, to front only the essential facts of life, and see if I could not learn what it had to teach, and not, when I came to die, to discover that I had not lived.

Henry David Thoreau

THIS IS A FAVORITE QUOTATION OF MINE. LIKE THOREAU, I WOULDN'T want to come to the end of life and find out that I had not lived. What a waste it would be not to use and enjoy God's gift of life to the fullest!

To get the most out of life, we have to do some spiritual exploring from time to time. Thoreau went to the woods so that he might live deliberately. At midlife, I had to go to an inner forest—a place of the mind and heart—and I invited you to go with me. In our inner forest, we unearthed questions, cleaned out the undergrowth of old issues, dug for answers, and nurtured new growth.

I don't know about you, but I'm ready to shout, "We did it!" Spiritual exploration takes courage and tenacity. If it hadn't been for Gwen and Saundra's letters—for their willingness to admit their struggles—I don't know if I would have found answers to my questions for lack of courage to try.

I'm not sure what happened with Gwen. Our letters became notes, and the time between them became longer and longer. Correspondence ceased altogether when she found a new job. She didn't see the process through, or at least with me she didn't.

But Saundra did. You know this because I have shared her story in this book. We went from letter-writing to phone conversations to numerous e-mails to discussing what was bothering us—looking for answers, sharing our visions, supporting each other, and praying together. The experience was so stimulating and energizing, I wonder now why I hesitated in the first place.

My connection with Saundra and with the many other women who contributed to this book has enabled me to see that we are women with choices. We can find answers that will change the quality of our middle years.

WOMEN WITH CHOICES

When Gwen and I were corresponding—when she was so indecisive about what she wanted to do—she closed one of her letters with, WHAT WILL I DO WITH THE REST OF MY LIFE? Her capital letters emphasized her angst and became the title for this book. Wondering if she resolved her dilemma, I e-mailed her one day. I asked, "Do you know now what you want to do with the rest of your life?"

She sent a brief message back: "My job is all right for now; it is keeping me occupied. As for what will I do with the rest of my life, I have no control over that. I don't think anybody does."

I disagree. It's true that we don't have total control—no one has that—but we have enough control to change the direction and the quality of our lives. My research, the surveys, the discussion groups, the e-mails, and my many candid conversations with middle-aged women have convinced me that we are able to make choices that will enable us to have decades more of purposeful living. It's up to us.

Urge to Surge

After looking back at where she had been and exploring goals for the future, Nancy, who works for a credit union, realizes she wants a more senior position in a related industry. She's now in the process of rearranging her life to do just that.

Tanya, though, wants out of corporate life. When she worked through the malaise she was experiencing, she knew she wanted a more meaningful job for her second adulthood. She's now searching for a job in the nonprofit sector—something where she is more concerned with changing lives than with profit margins.

Leigh thought her urge to surge had arrived when she took a job for the first time outside the home. She told everyone she was doing it to help with college bills as her children left; secretly, she wanted a regular job—one that counted, one with a paycheck and a retirement plan. But after two years on the job, when two of her daughters were having babies, she realized she wanted to be available for them. She quit her job. With enthusiasm and joy, she embraces her life as a mentor to her daughters and as an involved grandparent. Now she feels energized.

Sherry's midlife rebirth doesn't involve as much outward evidence as Nancy's, Tanya's, and Leigh's. Hers is a rebirth of the spirit. As she explored the spiritual questions of middlescence, she realized she had a thirst to know God in a more intimate way. Her early morning devotion times have lengthened, and her reading has deepened because her focus has changed.

In this book I invited you to join me in finding direction for your life by "living with" your questions and analyzing your reluctance to move into the future. We named feelings and traced their sources. I hope that in the process you looked at yourself and how others see you. My purpose in writing was to help you discover who you are, including discovering your strengths and who you want to become. My prayer for you has been that you have gained a sense of strength and power—that you are beginning to gain a vision for the kind of impact you can make in this world with God's help.

Simply put, I hope you have found answers to your questions—and if not, that you keep on exploring until you do!

While the end results appear very different, Nancy, Tanya, Leigh, and Sherry each found purpose, power, and peace. You can too. Your middle years can be productive, meaningful, and perhaps the greatest time of well-being in your life if you have a vision and pursue it.

DISCUSSION QUESTIONS

As you listen to the voices in this book, you may want to talk with or listen to what the women you know have to say. Invite some women to join you to "just talk," or organize your own middlescent discussion group. You may want to develop your own questions, or you can use those included here as discussion guidelines.

For my discussion groups, I mailed several questions to participants a week or two before our meeting. Sending them the questions ahead of time made for a richer time of sharing than springing the questions on them cold. Everyone could mull things over ahead of time and organize their thoughts. Most of the women brought written notes with them to the meeting.

We sat around a table, facing each other, and I asked each woman to respond to each question, covering one question at a time. This didn't mean we were formal or stiff or lacked spontaneity. Au contraire! We laughed, joked, interrupted each other, and sometimes got sidetracked. I allowed some digression to keep the conversation informal and lively, but after awhile I used the assigned questions to steer us back to the meeting's agenda. Using the questions guided our discussion, kept us on track, and helped the discussion to stay purposeful.

I used a circle response to ensure that everyone had a chance to talk. Every midlife woman has a story to share; a circle response keeps one person from dominating the discussion. Plus, we each got to see how all the others were feeling and what they were thinking and experiencing. By the time we concluded, we truly felt connected.

When I invited each participant, I told her our discussion would last between an hour to an hour and a half. Three or four questions, if prepared ahead of time, were all we could handle in that time frame. If you follow the guidelines for each week's discussion, you might want to select the four questions you think are best and assign those rather than trying to cover them all. If you don't assign the questions ahead of time, you may need more questions.

I think it's always important to conclude any discussion group with something positive. To do this, pull positive items or a recurrent theme from the participants' input. Or, if it lends itself, brainstorm together about specific ways to deal with the concerns mentioned, or close with selected meaningful passages from this book.

WEEK 1

READY, SET, GROW!

(Resource chapters: 1, 4, 5)
Middlescence is an invitation to grow and a challenge to change. Each woman's journey through this passage won't unfold in the same way, but it will be a call to growth.

1. Middlescence growth takes place in the mind, the heart, and the spirit. It begins with inner discontent, hazy fears, nagging questions, impulses, or pressure toward change; seeing ourselves, our roles, or others differently; disturbing dreams, or a sense that the old pattern no longer fits. Which of these have you experienced?
2. What spiritual questions are you asking?
3. What growing pains are you experiencing?
4. What hinders your growth?
5. How do relationships enrich a woman's life?
6. How might relationships hold a woman back from growing?
7. How does being healthy relate to growth?
8. Do physical problems eliminate the possibility of growth?
9. What changes can you make to facilitate your growth?

WEEK 2

REACHING FOR INNER HARMONY

(Resource chapters: 3, 6)
In a *Ladies' Home Journal* survey that reflected the demographics of the women in the United States, women from fifty-two to sixty-seven reported some major dissatisfactions. As they age,

they become increasingly lonely and worried about managing on their own. They're also more likely to be disappointed about the ways their lives turned out.[1]

1. What disturbs your inner harmony? What are some dissatisfactions you are currently experiencing?
2. What dreams and expectations did you have when you were in your twenties and thirties? How do you feel about those dreams and expectations now?
3. How will letting go of your past reveal possibilities for your future?
4. What things change when you accept what you cannot change?
5. What would give you more security as you age?
6. What would your life be like if you were freed from the fear of the future?
7. What would your life be like if you were freed from your fear of death?

Week 3

Tumbling Emotions by Day, Haunting Feelings by Night

(Resource chapter: 6)

Almost anything you pick up and read about women in midlife describes it as an emotional time. It is a time of change and challenges, and those kinds of things don't happen to us without our feelings getting involved. They seem to rumble around inside, residing in the background of our lives, while we go about our daily activities. At night, they disturb our sleep.

1. How do emotions enrich our lives?
2. What changes have you noticed in your emotions? Any emotional upheaval?
3. Are you experiencing emotions that are new *for you?* What varied emotions are you experiencing?
4. What are some possible explanations for your changing emotions?

5. When have you felt overwhelmed by your emotions?
6. How might emotions interfere with building a positive future?
7. Why is it important to release emotions? What happens when you release your emotions?
8. What are some healthy ways of releasing emotions?
9. How will taking action reduce feelings of helplessness?

WEEK 4

CRINGING AT THE THOUGHT

(Resource chapters: 2, 7, 8)
While some may be in crisis situations when signs of middle age begin appearing, most of us will be living comfortable lives. Our reaction to the approaching middle years may be resistance. We don't want to enter life's next stage or grow old.

1. Why do most of us resist moving to the next stage of life?
2. How old is old? At what age do you consider someone "old"?
3. Do you think society is prejudiced against the elderly? In what ways?
4. How prejudiced are you against the elderly? (If you are at a party or social, are you drawn toward conversation with the elderly, with young people, or with people your own age?)
5. What worries you the most about being old?
6. In what ways are all of us obsolete?
7. Are looks important as we grow older?
8. How can we resist our culture's pressure to be youthfully attractive?
9. How can we fight the fears of aging?
10. The Bible describes the virtuous woman as a "woman of strength and dignity" and with "no fear of old age" (Proverbs 31:25, TLB). How can we become like that woman?

WEEK 5

THE EMERGING POWER WOMAN

(Resource chapter: 9)
In her book *Jubilee Time*, Maria Harris writes, "The first half of life is over, and something new aches, even demands, to be born."[2] The growth pains of middlescence may be birth pains: a new woman, a new life, or a new power aching to be released.

1. Are you more yourself than you have ever been? Why or why not?
2. What are your strongest attributes?
3. What kinds of power do you observe and admire in other women over forty-five?
4. What are the gifts of your present stage of life that you have not experienced before?
5. How do you define power?
6. If power is the capacity to do and to act, in what ways are you powerful?
7. "Where is your power?"[3]
8. "Where is your powerlessness?"[3]
9. "Where does your powerlessness come from: yourself, society, others? What blocks are preventing you from claiming your power? How can you start disassembling these blocks?"[3]

WEEK 6

FAITH TO BECOME

(Resource chapters: 9, 12, 15)
A staying faith is a faith that comforts. It sustains us through life's unexpected turns and disappointments. We all want and need this kind of faith, but if we are to make the most of our middle years and have a purposeful life, we need more. We need faith to become the women God is calling us to be. We need a growing faith.

1. How would you contrast your present faith with the faith you had in your twenties and thirties?
2. What is something that your walk with God has taught you?

3. What if you revisited your youth group or your college Christian group, what kind of inner rumblings would it stir?
4. What does it mean to follow Christ without the vigor and idealism of youth?
5. If you could look at your faith objectively—see it as a muscle, for example—what would you need to do to strengthen your faith for the second half of life?
6. What meaning is there for the midlife woman in Jesus' words, "I am the resurrection and the life" (John 11:25)?
7. At midlife, why is it important to not only think about what we want but also to think about what God wants?

Week 7

The Eternal Connection

(Resource chapters: 11, 13)

The Bible says, "Honor God and obey his commands, because this is all people must do" (Ecclesiastes 12:13, NCV). Obedience is so basic to the Christian life that you would think we wouldn't even need to consider it at our age, but we do if we want meaningful lives.

1. What is there that makes having a sense of purpose so important? Why does meaning matter?
2. How are meaning and obedience related?
3. What midlife concerns challenge our obedience?
4. What freedoms do we gain through obedience?
5. What does recognizing our potential have to do with living meaningful lives?
6. Why might some middlescent women resist the idea of surrendering their self to God?
7. If we don't reconcile our wants with God's wants, what will we be missing?
8. How can we align our will with God's will?

Week 8

Come, Dream with Me

(Resource chapters: 9, 10, 14)

When a woman first enters the transitional waters of middlescence, she may feel as if she is paddling upstream, with her strokes meeting resistance. Her efforts will pick up momentum, however, when a vision begins forming in her mind of who she can be and what she can do.

1. If you could do anything you wanted to do, no holds barred, what would you do with the rest of your life?
2. Why are dreams important?
3. What do you want most to have accomplished or experienced before you die? Or, in the next ten years, what do you want to experience or accomplish?
4. What do you see yourself doing in the next ten to fifteen years?
5. Ten years from now, what kind of woman do you want to be?
6. How would you complete the statement "I am ________________"?
7. What is the difference in the following statements? Which one reflects your current attitude?
   "If only . . . "
   "I wish I had . . . "
   "What is . . . "
   "What if . . . "

Week 9

Dream-Building

(Resource chapters: 4, 14, 17)

A vision gives us an inner compass for our future. As one survey respondent expressed it, "It keeps our ship sailing in the right direction." A vision, though, does not guarantee a meaningful life. Life has a way of eroding dreams. The demands and expectations of others also press in on us. Even our own good intentions may get left by the wayside unless we commit ourselves to seeing our vision become reality.

1. What keeps visions from becoming reality?
2. Does it seem that others are preventing your dreams from coming true?
3. How can others help you pursue your dreams?
4. What is the difference between a dream in your head and a dream on paper?
5. How are dreams and goals related? How are they different?
6. What changes will you have to make to ensure that your dreams come true?
7. What is your dream for the future?
8. How can you turn your dreams into specific goals?
9. Why pursue goals if we have no guarantee that we will reach them?
10. How can I help others understand my dream?

WEEK 10

THE GIFT OF WISDOM

(Resource chapters: 9, 15, 16)
In one survey by *Parade* magazine, 75 percent of those surveyed said wisdom comes with age.[4] Wisdom is something many of us associate with aging.

1. What is something you know now that you didn't know when you were younger?
2. What is something that life has taught you?
3. How would you compare the wisdom you have now with the wisdom you had in your youth?
4. Do you anticipate growing wiser? How can you assure this will happen?
5. What are you no longer willing to keep silent about?
6. What are some ways we can use our wisdom?
7. How has "all that has gone before" been a preparation for what we can do and for what we can become?

Week 11

Leaving a Legacy

(Resource chapter: 16)

During middlescence, we begin wondering, *When I am gone, will anyone know I have been here? Will my life have counted? How will I be remembered? Will I have made a difference?* Leaving a legacy—making an impact—is important to us.

1. What is life asking of you?
2. What changes would you like to see made in the world around you?
3. Why is leaving a legacy important to us?
4. Why is our leaving a legacy important to God?
5. Why is it important to declare God's power to the next generation (see Psalm 71:18)? What are some ways we can do this?
6. How can we make an impact on our children and grandchildren?
7. How can we make an impact on younger women?

Week 12

Woman to Woman

(Resource chapter: 16)

The book of Titus is Paul's letter to a pastor by the name of Titus. In the letter, Paul advises Titus on how to teach the various groups of people in the church. We are interested in his instructions for "older women" (2:3-5) whom he said should teach and train the younger women.

1. What keeps older women from teaching younger women?
2. How would you rewrite Paul's instructions for "older women" in today's church?
3. What is the difference between being a role model for a younger woman and being her mentor?
4. Have you tried to be the woman in this passage? If yes, what kind of response did you receive from younger women?

5. If younger women don't want what we have to offer, does this negate the biblical mandate for older women?
6. What is a church missing when it doesn't encourage women to exercise the Titus 2 role?
7. What would you be missing if you didn't exercise this role?
8. If you could teach one thing to younger women, what would it be?
9. Who are your role models? Who are the "older women" in your life?

A SAMPLE OF THE SURVEY SENT TO WOMEN EXPERIENCING MIDDLESCENCE

I'm a NavPress author, and I need your help. I want to know the successes and the struggles of women ages 45 to 65 for a book I'm planning. I would appreciate your taking 20 to 30 minutes to answer the following questions. Your answers will provide valuable insight for other women. I'm looking for trends among the answers, so please be specific. Your answers will remain confidential. I will not quote you without your permission.

1. What do you enjoy most about your present age?

2. What kinds of power do you observe and admire in other women over 45? (For example: wisdom, independence, strong sense of self, etc.)

3. Have you made a positive change in your life since turning 45? (For example: "I went back to college," "I changed careers," "I started piano lessons," etc.)
   _____ yes (please go to question 4)
   _____ no (please go to question 5)

4. Please describe the change you made and then proceed to question 8.

5. Would you like to make a major change?
   _____ yes (please go to next question)
   _____ no (please skip to question 8)

6. What one change would you make?

7. What is keeping you from making that change?

8. To what do you want to commit yourself over the next ten to fifteen years? (For example: sustaining relationships,

developing the inner self, spiritual growth, gaining financial security, etc.)

9. What spiritual challenges have you faced (or are facing) since turning 45? (For example: a lackluster faith, floundering without purpose, dissatisfied with self, lack of inner peace, etc.)

10. Have any of these challenges influenced your answers on this survey?
    _____ yes (proceed to questions 11 & 12)
    _____ no (go to question 12)

11. Please describe how these challenges have influenced your answers.

12. What have you done (or are doing) to meet your spiritual challenges?

Please place a check mark on the line in front of the appropriate answer to each question.

13. I currently belong in the following age group:
    _____ 45-50 _____ 51-55 _____ 56-60 _____ 61-66

14. I am currently: _____ married _____ single
    _____ divorced _____ widowed

15. Children? _____ none _____ yes

Please return the survey in the enclosed self-addressed stamped envelope. Thank you for taking the time to consider and answer all of the survey questions.

Name ____

Street ____

City ____________________ State _________ Zip Code ____________

NOTES

Chapter 1

1. Paula Payne Hardin, *What Are You Doing with the Rest of Your Life?* (San Rafael, Calif.: New World Library, 1992), p. 3.
2. Marcia Lasswell and Thomas Lasswell, *Marriage and the Family* (Belmont, Calif.: Wadsworth Publishing Company, 1991), p. 474.
3. Joyce Rupp, *Dear Heart, Come Home: The Path of Midlife Spirituality* (New York: The Crossroad Publishing Company, 1996), p. 15.
4. Rupp, p. 16.
5. Douglas C. Kimmel, *Adulthood and Aging: An Interdisciplinary, Developmental View* (New York: Wiley, 1990), p. 104.
6. Kimmel, p. 104.
7. Hardin, p. 115.
8. Gail Sheehy, *New Passages* (New York: Random House, 1995), p. 140. Other authors have used similar terms: *The Spouse Gap: Weathering the Marriage Crisis During Middlessence* and *Middlescence: The Dangerous Years*.
9. Sheehy, p. 5.
10. Sheehy, pp. 5-6.
11. David J. Maitland, *Looking Both Ways: A Theology for Mid-Life* (Atlanta, Ga.: John Knox, 1985), p. ix.
12. A copy of the survey is found on pages 197-198 of this book.
13. Daniel J. Levinson, *The Seasons of a Man's Life* (New York: Knopf, 1978), p. 52.

Chapter 2

1. Gail Sheehy, *New Passages* (New York: Random House, 1995), pp. 59-60.
2. You may read more about Mildred Cable and Francesca and Evangeline French in *Guardians of the Great Commission* by Ruth Tucker (Grand Rapids, Mich.: Zondervan, 1988), pp. 81-88, and in *Something Happened* by Mildred Cable and Francesca French (London: Hodder and Stoughton, 1934).

Chapter 3

1. Bob Buford, *Half Time* (Grand Rapids, Mich.: Zondervan, 1994), p. 66.
2. Jim McGuiggan, *Jesus Hero of Thy Soul* (West Monroe, La.: Howard Publishing Co., 1998), p. 133.
3. Theologian Reinhold Niebuhr's Serenity Prayer, Martin E. P. Seligman, Ph.D., *What You Can Change and What You Can't* (New York: Knopf, 1994), p. vii. It is called "The Serenity Prayer" (1934), and is also attributed to Friedrich Oetinger (1702–1782).

4. Sarah Ban Breathnach, *Simple Abundance: A Daybook of Comfort and Joy* (New York: Warner Books, 1995), from January 23rd entry (n.p.).
5. Barbara Bartocci, "Let Go and Live," *Reader's Digest,* October 1989, p. 103.

Chapter 4

1. Paula B. Doress-Worters and Diana Laskin Siegal, *The New Ourselves, Growing Older: Women Aging with Knowledge and Power* (New York: Simon & Schuster, 1994), p. 133.
2. Ellen McGrath, Gwendolyn Puryear Keita, Bonnie R. Strickland, and Nancy Felipe Russo, *Women and Depression* (Washington, D.C.: American Psychological Association, 1990), pp. 24, 85-86.
3. Personal letter from Thelma Harris, October 12, 1998.
4. Doress-Worters and Laskin Siegal, p. 204.
5. David J. Maitland, *Looking Both Ways: A Theology for Mid-Life* (Atlanta, Ga.: John Knox, 1985), p. 3.
6. Catherine Marshall, *Something More* (New York: McGraw-Hill, 1974), p. 8.

Chapter 5

1. Eileen Hoffman, M.D., *Our Health, Our Lives* (New York: Simon & Schuster, 1995), p. 248.
2. Paula Span, "Learning to Love Menopause," *Good Housekeeping,* June 1997, p. 81.
3. The Boston Women's Health Book Collective, *The New Our Bodies, Ourselves* (New York: Simon & Schuster, 1992), p. 517.
4. Personal letter from Peggy Brooks, November 5, 1994.
5. Hoffman, p. 251.
6. Associated Press article in the *Times-Mail*, Bedford, Ind., October 14, 1998, p. 112.
7. Leslie Laurence, "What Women Must Know *Before* Menopause," *Reader's Digest*, October 1994, p. 112.
8. Laurence, p. 112.
9. E. Stanley Jones, *Victory Through Surrender* (Nashville, Tenn.: Abingdon, 1966), p. 110.
10. E-mail message from Peggy Brooks, November 6, 1998.

Chapter 6

1. Ellen McGrath, Ph.D., *When Feeling Bad Is Good* (New York: Henry Holt and Company, 1992), p. 171.
2. Daniel J. Levinson, *The Seasons of a Woman's Life* (New York: Knopf, 1996), p. 175.

Chapter 7

1. From Malcolm Boyd, *Rich with Years* (New York: HarperCollins, 1994), as quoted in *Virtue,* July/August 1994, p. 42.
2. Letty Cottin Pogrebin, *Getting Over Getting Older* (New York: Little, Brown, 1996), p. 131.

3. The Boston Women's Health Book Collective, *The New Our Bodies, Ourselves* (New York: Simon & Schuster, 1992), p. 521.
4. Ellen McGrath, Ph. D., *When Feeling Bad Is Good* (New York: Henry Holt and Company, 1992), p. 224.
5. Pogrebin, p. 149.
6. Bernie Siegel, M.D., *Peace, Love and Healing* (New York: Harper & Row, 1989), p. 30.
7. Siegel, pp. 31, 32, 33.
8. The Boston Women's Health Book Collective, p. 521.

Chapter 8

1. Laura Alden and Dr. Carol Pierskalla, "Aging Today and Tomorrow," *The American Baptist,* September 1991, p. 17.
2. E-mail message from Athalene, a survey respondent, March 17, 1998.
3. This exercise was described in my book *Why Do I Feel This Way?* (Colorado Springs, Colo.: NavPress, 1996), pp. 157-158.
4. Joyce Brothers, *Positive Plus* (New York: Putnam, 1994), p. 74.
5. Gail Sheehy, *New Passages* (New York: Random House, 1995), p. 233.
6. Ellen McGrath, Ph.D., *When Feeling Bad Is Good* (New York: Henry Holt and Company, 1992), pp. 174-175.
7. McGrath, p. 175.
8. E-mail message from Athalene, March 17, 1998.

Chapter 9

1. Eugenia Price, *St. Simons Memoir* (New York: J. B. Lippincott, 1978), p. 41.
2. Ruth Formanek, Ph.D., "Depression and the Older Woman," *Women and Depression: A Lifespan Perspective* (New York: Springer, 1987), p. 279.
3. Ellen McGrath, Ph.D., *When Feeling Bad Is Good* (New York: Henry Holt and Company, 1992), p. 178.
4. Gail Sheehy, *New Passages* (New York: Random House, 1995), p. 327.
5. Joan Borysenko, Ph.D., *A Woman's Book of Life* (New York: Riverhead Books, 1996), pp. 148, 158.
6. Sheehy, p. 327.
7. Colette Dowling, *Red Hot Mamas: Coming Into Our Own at Fifty* (New York: Bantam, 1996), p. 14.
8. Eileen Hoffman, M.D., *Our Health, Our Lives* (New York: Simon & Schuster, 1995), p. 249.
9. Author's paraphrase of words from the traditional African-American song, "Free at Last."
10. Dowling, p. 13.
11. Personal correspondence with Athalene, a survey respondent, July 29, 1997.

Chapter 10

1. Psalm 90:10,12 (TEV)

2. Marcia Lasswell and Thomas Lasswell, *Marriage and the Family* (Belmont, Calif.: Wadsworth Publishing Company, 1991), p. 474.
3. Rachel Naomi Remen, *Kitchen Table Wisdom* (New York: Riverhead Books, 1996), p. 93.
4. Letty Cottin Pogrebin, *Getting Over Getting Older* (New York: Little, Brown, 1996), p. 5.
5. Douglas C. Kimmel, *Adulthood and Aging: An Interdisciplinary, Developmental View* (New York: Wiley, 1990), pp. 527-528.
6. Ellen McGrath, Ph.D., *When Feeling Bad Is Good* (New York: Henry Holt and Company, 1992), pp. 179-180.
7. Remen, p. 172.

Chapter 11

1. Jan Johnson, *Living a Purpose-Full Life* (Colorado Springs, Colo.: WaterBrook Press, 1999), pp. 66-73.

Chapter 12

1. James Rodney Bolejack, "An Assessment of the Use of Selected Developmental Issues As Teachable Experiences for Faith Enrichment in Middle-Age Adults" (Ph.D. diss., Southwestern Baptist Theological Seminary, 1988), p. 93.
2. Bolejack, p. 94.
3. Laura Alden and Dr. Carol Pierskalla, "Aging Today and Tomorrow," *The American Baptist*, September 1991, p. 18.

Chapter 13

1. E. Stanley Jones, *Victory Through Surrender* (Nashville, Tenn.: Abingdon, 1966), p. 27.
2. Author's "loose translation" and summary of the messages of Isaiah, Jeremiah, Hosea, Amos, Micah, Habakkuk, Zephaniah, Haggai, Zechariah, and Malachi.
3. William Barclay, *The Letters to the Philippians, Colossians and Thessalonians* (Edingurgh: The Saint Andrew Press, 1960).
4. Jones, p. 33.

Chapter 14

1. Clarence Jordan, *Cotton Patch Version of Hebrews and The General Epistles* (New York: Association Press, 1973).
2. Joyce Brothers, *Positive Plus* (New York: Putnam, 1994), p. 87.

Chapter 15

1. Marlene LeFever and Karen Mains, "Eight Questions to Ask on Your Next Birthday," *Discipleship Journal*, Issue 74, 1993, p. 67.
2. As quoted by Ellen McGrath, Ph. D., *When Feeling Bad Is Good* (New York: Henry Holt and Company, 1992), p. 174.
3. Stephen L. Carter, *Integrity* (New York: Basic Books, HarperCollins, 1996), pp. 7, 10.
4. Gladys Hunt, "Let's Live Creatively!" *Moody Monthly*, May 1974, p. 52.

Chapter 16

1. Susan Hunt, *Spiritual Mothering: The Titus 2 Model for Women Mentoring Women* (Franklin, Tenn.: Legacy Communications, 1992), p. 44.
2. Clare Ansberry, "A Kansas Woman Pens Her Memoir and Finds, At Last, Redemption," *Wall Street Journal,* March 7, 1997, p. A1.
3. Ansberry, p. A6.

Chapter 17

1. May Sarton, *At Seventy: A Journal* (New York: Norton, 1984), p. 10, as quoted in Holly W. Whitcomb, *Feasting with God: Adventures in Table Spirituality* (Cleveland, Ohio: United Church Press, 1996), p. 32.
2. Letty Cottin Pogrebin, *Getting Over Getting Older* (New York: Little, Brown, 1996), p. 7.
3. Frances Weaver, *The Girls with the Grandmother Faces* (New York: Hyperion, 1996), p. 38.
4. Weaver, pp. 47-48.
5. Weaver, p. 48.
6. Susan Hunt, *Spiritual Mothering: The Titus 2 Model for Women Mentoring Women* (Franklin, Tenn.: Legacy Communications, 1992), pp. 73-90.
7. Anna Roufos, "What's Hot & What's Not," *Ladies' Home Journal,* February 1998, p. 98.

Discussion Questions

1. "American Women: Where We Are Now," *Ladies' Home Journal,* September 1997, p. 132.
2. Maria Harris, *Jubilee Time* (New York: Bantam, 1995), p. 2.
3. Holly W. Whitcomb, *Feasting with God: Adventures in Table Spirituality* (Cleveland, Ohio: United Church Press, 1996), p. 33.
4. Mark Clements, "What Do We Say About Aging?" *Parade,* December 12, 1993, p. 5.

BIBLIOGRAPHY

Ansberry, Clare. "A Kansas Woman Pens Her Memoir and Finds, At Last, Redemption," *Wall Street Journal*, March 7, 1997, pp. A1 and A6.

Austin, Elizabeth. "The Secret to Midlife Health," *McCall's*, May 1994, pp. 56, 58, 64, 65, 158.

Bartocci, Barbara. "Let Go and Live," *Reader's Digest*, October 1989, p. 103.

Bartocci, Barbara. *Midlife Awakenings: Discovering the Gifts Life Has Given Us*. Notre Dame, Indiana: Ave Maria Press, 1998.

Bolejack, James Rodney. "An Assessment of the Use of Selected Developmental Issues as Teachable Experiences for Faith Enrichment in Middle-Age Adults." Ph.D. diss. Southwestern Baptist Theological Seminary, 1988.

Borysenko, Joan. *A Woman's Book of Life: The Biology, Psychology, and Spirituality of the Feminine Life Cycle*. New York: Riverhead Books, 1996.

The Boston Women's Health Book Collective. *The New Our Bodies, Ourselves: A Book by and for Women*. New York: Simon & Schuster, 1992.

Brothers, Dr. Joyce. "Are You Caught in the Middle?" *Parade*, June 28, 1998, pp. 4, 5, 7.

Brothers, Joyce. *Positive Plus*. New York: Putnam, 1994.

Buford, Bob. *Halftime: Changing Your Game Plan from Success to Significance*. Grand Rapids, Michigan: Zondervan Publishing House, 1994.

Calvo, Trisha. "Hot Flash! Is It Menopause—Already?" *McCall's*, December 1998, pp. 78, 79, 82, 83.

Denny, Dann. "Unconditional . . . a mother's love," *Sunday Herald-Times*, May 30, 1999, p. F1.

Doress-Worters, Paula B., and Diana Laskin Siegal. *The New Ourselves, Growing Older: Women Aging with Knowledge and Power*. New York: A Touchstone Book published by Simon and Schuster, 1987, 1994.

Dowling, Colette. *Red Hot Mamas: Coming Into Our Own at Fifty*. New York: Bantam Books, 1996.

Formanek, Ruth, and Anita Gurian, eds. *Women and Depression: A Lifespan Perspective*. New York: Springer, 1987.

Hardin, Paula Payne. *What Are You Doing With the Rest of Your Life?*. San Rafael, California: New World Library, 1992, p. 3.

Harris, Maria. *Jubilee Time: Celebrating Women, Spirit, and the Advent of Age*. New York: Bantam Books, 1995.

Hoffman, M.D., Eileen. *Our Health, Our Lives*. New York: Simon & Schuster, 1995.

Hunt, Susan. *Spiritual Mothering: The Titus 2 Model for Women Mentoring Women*. Franklin, Tennessee: Legacy Communications, 1992.

Jacoby, Susan. "The Hidden Stress That Really Hurts," *McCall's*, February 1998, pp. 85, 86, 87, 90.

Johnson, Jan. *Living A Purpose-Full Life*. Colorado Springs, Colorado: WaterBrook Press, 1999.

Jones, E. Stanley. *Victory Through Surrender*. Nashville, Tennessee: Abingdon Press, 1966.

Kerns, Virginia, and Judith K. Brown, eds. *In Her Prime: New Views of Middle-Aged Women*. Urbana and Chicago: University of Illinois Press, 1992.

Kimmel, Douglas C. *Adulthood and Aging: An Interdisciplinary, Developmental View,* New York: John Wiley & Sons, 1990.

Konitzer, Martha J. "A New Wrinkle on Aging," *Virtue*, February March, 1999, pp. 40, 41, 42.

Levinson, Daniel J. *The Seasons of a Woman's Life*. New York: Alfred A. Knopf, 1996.

LeFever, Marlene, and Karen Mains. "Eight Questions to Ask on Your Next Birthday," *Discipleship Journal*, Issue Seventy-Four, 1993, pp. 66, 67, 68.

Laurence, Leslie. "The Baby-boomer Health Guide: What's Happening to Me?" *Ladies' Home Journal*, April 1994, pp. 73, 74, 76, and 78.

Maitland, David J. *Looking Both Ways: A Theology for Mid-Life*. Atlanta, Georgia: John Knox Press, 1985.

McGrath, Ph.D., Ellen. *When Feeling Bad Is Good*. New York: Henry Holt and Company, 1992.

McGrath, Ellen; Gwendolyn Puryear Keita; Bonnie R. Strickland; and Nancy Felipe Russo. *Women and Depression*. Washington, D.C.: American Psychological Association, 1990.

Murray, Mary. "The Female Secret to Living Longer," *McCall's*, November 1994, pp. 52, 58, 60, 62, 63.

Parker, Dr. William R., and Elaine St. Johns. *Prayer Can Change Your Life*. New York: Simon & Schuster, 1957.

Pogrebin, Letty Cottin. *Getting Over Getting Older: An Intimate Journey*. New York: Little, Brown and Company, 1996.

Remen, Rachel Naomi. *Kitchen Table Wisdom*. New York: Riverhead Books, 1996.

Rupp, Joyce. *Dear Heart, Come Home: The Path of Midlife Spirituality*. New York: The Crossroad Publishing Company, 1996.

Schechter, Bruce. "Why Time Flies. . . and How to Slow it Down," *Reader's Digest*, January 1992, pp. 13-16.

Sheehy, Gail. *New Passages*. New York: Random House, 1995.

Span, Paula. "Learning to Love Menopause," *Good Housekeeping*, June 1997, pp. 81, 82, 83, 89.

Tournier, Paul. *The Seasons of Life,* trans John S. Gilmour, Richmond, Virginia: John Knox Press, 1963.

Weaver, Frances. *The Girls with the Grandmother Faces*. New York: Hyperion, 1996.

Worters, Paula B., and Diana Laskin Siegal. *The New Ourselves, Growing Older: Women Aging with Knowledge and Power*. New York: A Touchstone Book published by Simon and Schuster, 1987, 1994.

ABOUT THE AUTHOR

The conversations that prompted Brenda Poinsett to write this book continue. She meets many women over age forty-five who want to talk. They have stories to tell, struggles to share, and triumphs to celebrate. To give them an opportunity, Brenda has moved from small-group discussions and surveys to retreats.

Are you asking yourself, *What will I do with the rest of my life?* Come, dream with other women at small, Brenda-led retreats in the Midwest. In an interactive environment you will discover God's best for you.

Or invite Brenda to dream with you as a speaker and/or discussion leader at your church, conference, or retreat.

You may contact Brenda by writing to NavPress at PO Box 35001, Colorado Springs, Colorado, 80935.